JUST
COOK IT!

JUST
COOK IT!

145 BUILT-TO-BE-EASY RECIPES
THAT ARE TOTALLY DELICIOUS

JUSTIN CHAPPLE

PHOTOGRAPHY BY DAVID MALOSH

Houghton Mifflin Harcourt
BOSTON / NEW YORK / 2018

For information about permission to reproduce selections from this book, write to trade.permissions@hmhco.com or to Permissions, Houghton Mifflin Harcourt Publishing Company, 3 Park Avenue, 19th Floor, New York, New York 10016.

hmhco.com

Library of Congress Cataloging-in-Publication Data
Names: Chapple, Justin, author.
Title: Just cook it! : 145 built-to-be-easy recipes that are totally delicious / Justin Chapple. Description: Boston: Houghton Mifflin Harcourt, 2018. | Includes index.
Identifiers: LCCN 2017059030 (print) | LCCN 2017051913 (ebook) | ISBN 9780544968851 (ebook) | ISBN 9780544968837 (paper over board) Subjects: LCSH: Quick and easy cooking. | LCGFT: Cookbooks. Classification: LCC TX833.5 (print) | LCC TX833.5 .C433 2018 (ebook) | DDC 641.5/12—dc23

LC record available at https://lccn.loc.gov/2017059030

Cover and interior design by Laura Palese

Food styling by Barrett Washburne

Prop styling by Ayesha Patel

Printed in China

TOP 10 9 8 7 6 5 4 3 2 1

FOR
**GRANDMA
BARBARA**

CONTENTS

INTRODUCTION

Don't tell anyone, but I might've been a little bit dorky as a kid (not that I've changed much). I was freckly and quirky with all sorts of big, bizarre dreams. I would read cookbooks and food magazines, watch *Two Fat Ladies* and *Yan Can Cook!* on TV, and fantasize about becoming a chef.

Yes, a chef! That may have seemed like a stretch for a boy who grew up eating boxed mac and cheese, but that's what I wanted.

I graduated from The French Culinary Institute in Manhattan, then landed a gig working the line at a fancy restaurant. And then, in a "pinch me" moment, I got a job at *Food & Wine*. Today, in the *F&W* Test Kitchen, I do everything from create recipes to invent wonderfully oddball kitchen hacks for my video series, *Mad Genius Tips*. I even get to cook on television and in front of live audiences.

At *F&W*, I'm often tasked with taking recipes developed by chefs and simplifying them for the home cook. That might mean trimming a ridiculously long ingredient list, coming up with a clever shortcut so a dish doesn't take twelve hours to make, or tweaking a method so it's essentially foolproof. I promise, I'm totally humble, but I've become quite the expert. After years of adapting recipes from superstar chefs like Thomas Keller and David Chang, I know when you really have to sift the flour or peel the tomatoes and when it's okay to skip that step. I know when a soup needs to be strained and when it's perfectly delicious as is.

Still, if you ask me, you can't do this kind of work well unless you understand how people really cook at home. And that was the lesson of my entire childhood. I grew up in Stockton, California, in the agriculturally rich Central Valley, with two brothers, three sisters, lots of cousins, and loads of nieces and nephews. It seemed like our refrigerator door was always open. We didn't have much money, but we lived sensibly and had our own tricks for making food more affordable.

My grandma Barbara, for instance, would create incredible meals practically out of thin air. She'd doctor instant ramen with all kinds of flavorings, then zap it in the microwave; transform eggs, an inexpensive staple of our diet, into a kind of homespun soufflé; and churn ice cream in a blender that was forever on its last leg. She didn't give these recipes formal names. Instead, she just cooked with what little she had, and we ate it.

Looking back, I'm blown away by how much my grandma accomplished. I think she knew her food was delicious, but not how much fun I thought it was, or how much it inspired me. Sometimes I wish so hard that I could go back in time and tell her that I paid attention, even if it seemed like no one else in the world did, and thank her. Though my skills have improved since I left home and went to culinary school—seriously, my tuna salad has come a very long way—my grandma made me the cook I am today.

Because I'm a nostalgic person, I've filled this book with reinventions of my childhood favorites as well as faster versions of the classic dishes—Caesar salad, beef bourguignon, lasagna—so many of us crave. Over the years it's become clear to me that home cooks (ahem, this means you!) are far savvier than they're usually given credit for. So while all my recipes are no-fuss and reliable to their core, they will push you to think in new ways. The food in *Just Cook It!* is creative, fresh, surprising, often healthy, and always delicious.

I became a professional cook because I'm crazy about food and love to feed others. When I worked in restaurants, the job was stimulating and rigorous, but just a bit unfulfilling because I wasn't interacting with the people who were eating what I made. Since then, I've had the opportunity to gain what I was missing. And no, I'm not talking about the extra pounds around my waist, but rather the experience of connecting with my audience. Whether I've met you at an event or communicated with you through Facebook, Twitter, or Instagram, it's been all sorts of incredible. I love it! And I thank you for it.

So, just to be sure we're all on the same page, can we agree that we all want to prepare tasty and impressive recipes? That we love to entertain, be entertained, and cook for fun? That we appreciate oldies but goodies even if ultimately we want versions that are easier and oh so modern? I wrote this book because I know we're all looking for uncomplicated recipes that work every time, and that are exciting and new. I wrote this book for you. So just cook it!

"JUST COOK IT!"
PANTRY

None of the recipes in this book require crazy, weird, or expensive ingredients. I play with novel flavors all day in the *Food & Wine* Test Kitchen so when I go home, I mostly want to cook with what I have on hand. Here's how to stock your pantry just like mine so you can make any recipe in this book as well as create some of your own dishes along the way.

OIL

CANOLA OR VEGETABLE OIL

These two mild-tasting oils are pretty interchangeable. Use them to dress salads with subtle flavors or to sauté ingredients over high heat.

EXTRA-VIRGIN OLIVE OIL

The "good for you" oil is far more flavorful than canola or vegetable. It's great for dressings and any type of cooked recipe that requires low or medium heat. Not all brands are created equal, so do your research to be sure you're getting one that's pure. I like California Olive Ranch and Frantoia from Sicily.

TOASTED SESAME OIL

This oil can lend a wonderful nuttiness to dressings and cooked foods. The flavor is intense, so a little goes a long way. It can go rancid quickly, so buy the freshest bottle you can and store it in a cool spot in the pantry or even in the fridge.

SALT & PEPPER

KOSHER SALT

If you only keep one salt in the pantry, make it this one. Why? Kosher salt is coarser than table salt (you know, that iodized stuff) and is easy to pick up between your fingers, ultimately giving you more control. Keep in mind that kosher salt is "fluffier" than table salt, so even if you feel like you're using too much, you're probably not. I recommend Diamond Crystal because the flakes dissolve quickly.

FLAKY SEA SALT

Ideal for finishing dishes that benefit from a crunchy, salty bite, like open-face sandwiches and even chocolate pudding or ice cream. I happen to love the Maldon brand from England because it's widely available and has big, flavorful crystals. Another great one is the hand-harvested sea salt from Jacobsen Salt Co. in Oregon.

BLACK PEPPER

Always grind black peppercorns yourself with a pepper mill. Preground black pepper gets musty quickly and doesn't have much flavor. Also, avoid buying mixed peppercorns because, believe it or not, they're often packed with filler, like allspice berries.

WHITE PEPPER

Best for any food that might look better without little black specks in it, like my Whipped Feta Dip (page 36). I also like to use it in Asian recipes because it sometimes can mimic the tingling sensation of Sichuan peppercorns.

VINEGAR

CHAMPAGNE VINEGAR

My go-to vinegar. I love its bright acidity, especially in vinaigrettes.

RED WINE VINEGAR

It has a fuller flavor than champagne vinegar. I prefer it for cooking.

RICE VINEGAR

Slightly sweet but also mild, it's similar to champagne vinegar but without the winey edge. It's my favorite for pickling fruits and vegetables and is also great for marinades and dressings.

APPLE CIDER VINEGAR

Fruity and pungent, it's perfect with other strong-tasting ingredients, like cabbage or mushrooms, and also pairs well with meats.

DISTILLED WHITE VINEGAR

It's not just for household cleaning! This is probably the strongest vinegar of all, so use it sparingly. Stir a tablespoon or two into a soup or stew that just needs "a little something extra."

SPICES

CARAWAY SEEDS

The secret to everything from sublime roasted chicken to my Smoked Salmon Rillettes (page 44).

CELERY SEEDS

These tiny seeds can add a concentrated burst of flavor to dressings, slaws, and even savory pastries. Oh, and they can be used to rim the glass for a Bloody Mary.

CORIANDER

I keep ground coriander in the pantry, but I much prefer the whole seeds, which I crush myself. They have an intense fruity flavor and lend a brilliant crunchy texture to so many foods—even fried eggs.

CUMIN

Ground cumin is ideal when you want a funky, smoky punch. Cumin seeds, which taste a little sweeter, benefit from toasting, so they're fun sautéed with other aromatics.

CURRY POWDER

You won't typically find this powder in a real Indian curry because it's actually a Western approximation of spice blends used in Indian cuisine, which vary from region to region and even from cook to cook. But its inauthenticity is actually what I love about it. I appreciate the depth and spice it adds to my recipes. Buy Madras curry powder if you can find it.

GARLIC & ONION POWDERS

They are no substitute for the real thing, but their toasty, sweet flavors can add a lot to dressings, marinades, and rubs.

PAPRIKA

Hungarian-style sweet and hot paprikas and Spanish-style smoked paprika (sweet or hot) are essential. All are made from dried red peppers, but the smoked kind has a particularly intense flavor.

TOASTED SESAME SEEDS

I keep a big jar in the freezer, where it will last forever. Untoasted white sesame seeds can be found on the regular ol' spice aisle, but look for toasted ones in the Asian section of the grocery store.

TURMERIC POWDER

This ground root adds earthy flavor to stews and sautés and a gorgeous orange color to dips and soups.

VANILLA EXTRACT

Any extract that isn't pure is pretty much a waste of money. The imitation kind should be banned. I prefer to buy Nielsen-Massey brand but Rodelle is lovely, too.

HOT & SPICY FOODS

ASIAN CHILE SAUCES

Sriracha is my all-purpose favorite. It's lightly sweet, with a fresh chile flavor and a hit of garlic. Sambal oelek (either the classic version made with just red chiles, vinegar, and salt, or the garlic-spiked kind) is delicious in soups and sauces or spooned onto steamed rice. Gochujang, the fermented Korean hot pepper paste, is deeply savory and pungent, with a serious chile flavor.

LOUISIANA-STYLE HOT SAUCES

These are very spicy and tangy because they're made with so much vinegar. Use Tabasco, Crystal, or Frank's RedHot brands for any food that can handle a fiery kick—from chicken wings to popcorn.

MEXICAN-STYLE HOT SAUCES

These always remind me of being a kid because we used them so much. Brands like Cholula or Tapatío tend to be slightly smoky, with more body than the Louisiana-style sauces.

CHILE POWDER

I rely on everyday chili powder (spelled with an "i"), which is a blend of spices, as well as pure chile powders (spelled with an "e"), like ancho and chipotle. They're pretty interchangeable, but the pure stuff often adds a sweeter and sometimes spicier flavor that you'll notice more and more as you incorporate it into your cooking.

CHIPOTLES IN ADOBO

These smoked jalapeños in adobo sauce are crazy hot, so be sure to remove the seeds to tame the fire. The sauce can be used just like the chiles because it's infused with all that heat. Freeze extra in a resealable baggie.

KIMCHI

Keep a jar of this pungent Korean condiment in the refrigerator to make easy soup (page 91) or to eat as a healthy snack. It's available at most stores in the refrigerated section—

look by the sauerkraut or tofu. You can puree it into dips or finely chop it and add it to salad dressings, too.

FLOURS, GRAINS & STUFF THAT'S SIMILAR

FLOUR

All-purpose flour is a must for everything from breading to baking, but I also recommend keeping a small bag of whole wheat flour in the freezer (it'll last longer in there). You should also keep corn flour (aka cornmeal) on hand. I prefer masa harina, from Mexico, because it has the strongest corn flavor.

DRIED POTATO FLAKES

Also known as instant mashed potatoes. I use them in place of bread crumbs for coating fish and meat when I have guests who prefer to eat gluten-free. Check out my trout schnitzel (page 192) to learn how.

RICE & GRAINS

Long-grain white rice is the most versatile; my favorites are jasmine and basmati, which are similar enough to stand in for each other. Other essential grains are quinoa and farro.

For something a little more interesting, substitute freekeh (roasted green wheat) in any recipe that calls for farro.

FROZEN PUFF PASTRY

All you have to do is thaw puff pastry and it's ready to bake. You can make pastries, pizza, and even fruit tarts without opening a bag of flour.

BROTHS, SAUCES & MILKS

CHICKEN BROTH

Keep it on hand *at all times*. Buy low-sodium versions because they give you more control over the level of salt in your dish. Avoid brands that use a lot of vegetables because they tend to be sweeter, which distracts from the chicken taste. If you can find a brand that is made with chicken fat (aka schmaltz) it's probably packed with flavor. I like Natural Goodness from Swanson.

CLAM JUICE

Rather than buying fish stock, which can be very inconsistent brand to brand, I substitute clam juice. My favorite is Bar Harbor.

MARINARA SAUCE

Buy Rao's if you can, or another brand that uses extra-virgin olive oil and fresh garlic, onion, and other ingredients. Try to avoid ones that have a lot of added sugar.

SWEETENED CONDENSED MILK

I pretty much always have a can of this in the pantry for when I want to make anything from almost-instant ice cream to hot chocolate.

UNSWEETENED COCONUT MILK

Not only do I keep this on hand to make killer curries and soups, but also for Thai-spiced hot chocolate (page 262). Avoid "lite" versions because they are tasteless.

VEGETABLES

ARTICHOKES

The frozen ones are easy to use and full of flavor. Just defrost them and they're ready to go.

BEETS

I keep a package of steamed beets in the fridge and a jar of pickled ones in the pantry. I use them on open-face sandwiches (page 55), in dips (page 37), and for fast soups (page 106).

HEARTS OF PALM

Keep a jar or can on hand for salads. I also use them to cut the calories in bean dips (page 41) and hummus.

PEAS

You literally never need to buy fresh peas because the frozen ones are so delicious.

PEPPERS

When it comes to jarred peppers, roasted red ones are usually way too soft and watery-tasting. A few alternatives: Piquillos from Spain are tender, sweet, and delicious. Peppadews, pickled peppers from South Africa, are sold as sweet or spicy. Hot cherry peppers add a bright, very spicy flavor to creamy sauces and even pan-roasted meats.

CONDIMENTS

ASIAN FISH SAUCE

This very intense sauce adds a pungent dose of umami to anything. Learn to love this and you'll discover a whole new world of cooking.

CURRY PASTE

Packed with green chile, garlic, lemongrass, galangal (aka Thai ginger), and makrut lime, green curry paste is essential for salads, stir-fries, and even chicken soups. Red curry paste is also a must.

DIJON MUSTARD

I use it almost as much as I use champagne vinegar. I buy the biggest jar of Maille Dijon Originale I can find.

MAYONNAISE

There are plenty of reasons to love it, if you don't already. It can transform any vinaigrette into a creamy dressing and serve as the base for all kinds of dips and sauces. Buy Hellmann's (if you're east of the Rockies) or Best Foods (if you live out West).

MUST-HAVE EQUIPMENT

Seriously, having the right equipment is the first and best way to set yourself up for cooking success. Skip all those one-trick ponies and get some basic tools that can do double, triple, or quadruple duty.

COOKWARE

BAKING DISHES

These can be ceramic (my choice) or glass. Always have a 9 by 13-inch version (rectangle and/or oval) as well as a small (about 1 quart) and a medium (1½ to 2 quarts).

BAKING SHEETS

I don't have too much space in my apartment, so I use large rimmed sheets for all my baking needs. Usually, they're 13 by 18 inches and have a rim that's anywhere from ½ to 1 inch high. Cookie sheets are nice (they let heat circulate around cookies because they don't have a rim) but baking sheets work harder.

CAKE PANS

I don't use cake pans too often. Except when making cakes—go figure! You should try to have 8- and 9-inch pans. With that in mind, you should also get a springform pan that is either 8 or 9 inches in diameter. It'll make my No-Bake Cheesecake (page 254) a cinch.

CAST-IRON PANS

As an apartment dweller, I highly recommended a cast-iron grill pan for simulating a grill indoors. Also, you definitely need a large (12-inch) cast-iron skillet for getting the perfect char on thin steaks or when you want your skillet to double as a heat-retaining serving dish.

LOAF PAN

Get a 9 by 5-inch metal one to use for meat loaf (page 230) and homemade breads.

MUFFIN PAN

Because muffins and cupcakes and breakfast buns (page 71).

PIE PLATES

Use 8- and 9-inch pie plates for making pies, of course, but also for toasting nuts or bread crumbs and even in place of a shallow bowl for breading chicken cutlets or fish.

SAUCEPANS

You should keep small, medium, and large stainless-steel saucepans. Small saucepans range from 1- to 1½ quarts. Medium ones should be about 3 quarts, and large sizes can be 7 to 8 quarts. It's nice to have one medium nonstick saucepan, but think of that as a luxury.

SKILLETS

You really only need one large (12-inch) nonstick skillet. An ovenproof model will handle all your nonstick-skillet needs. You should also have a small (about 6-inch), medium (8- to 10-inch), and large (12- to 14-inch) stainless-steel skillet. Plus, you'll want either a large, deep skillet (12 inches wide and 2 inches deep) or a large enameled cast-iron braiser for cooking foods that require a good amount of liquid.

STEAMER BASKET

Yep, you should have one of those old-school collapsible models. They outperform all those weird sold-on-TV pieces of steaming equipment and are easy to store. Just be sure to have one with little feet to hold it up off the bottom of the pan. I use mine for steaming veggies and dumplings, like my shumai (page 56).

COUNTERTOP EQUIPMENT

BLENDER

I trust you have one already, but if not, get one quick! I don't like the models that have preset buttons for soup or sauce or chopping, though I do like the ones that automatically shut off after pureeing for a preset amount of time. If you can, buy a blender that has a *very* shallow cup at the bottom so all your food won't get stuck in there—that's the worst!

FOOD PROCESSOR

Not too many of my recipes require a food processor, but I highly recommend that you invest in one for pureeing, chopping, and shredding. It will change the way you cook forever. Don't splurge on some crazy, fancy model that does a billion things—stick with a basic one. I trust KitchenAid, Cuisinart, and Breville brands.

ELECTRIC HANDHELD MIXER

They've been around forever for a reason—they work! My choice is a KitchenAid 9-speed handheld mixer because it's powerful and lightweight.

MORTAR & PESTLE

I don't specify to use this in the book, but I think you should get one. It makes crushing seeds, like coriander and cumin, easier. I keep one on the counter and use it every time I roast chicken. Marble ones are beautiful, but unpolished granite ones are more effective.

SLOW COOKER

I just want to remind you how awesome they are. All-Clad sells my favorite, but whichever you choose, make sure it's 6 to 7 quarts.

DISPOSABLE STUFF

PLASTIC BAGGIES

Always have 1-quart and 1-gallon baggies on hand. They are, by far, the best way to store anything ever. Plus, if you buy BPA-free bags, you can even cook in them. I buy 2-gallon bags when I need to marinate big roasts or store huge heads of lettuce or cabbage.

ALUMINUM FOIL

Do yourself a favor and buy *large* heavy-duty foil. You can use it create an easy-cleanup work surface or to cover an entire baking sheet seamlessly. Plus, it won't tear easily.

PARCHMENT & WAXED PAPER

These papers are so insanely useful. Parchment is super nonstick and can be baked, while waxed paper is ideal for projects that don't require heat but benefit from a nonstick surface. Why have both? Waxed paper is way cheaper than parchment!

KNIVES

BREAD KNIFE

The long, serrated blade is great not just for slicing bread without squishing it, but for cutting sandwiches (ahem, BLTs) in half.

CHEF'S KNIFE

Besides your hands, this is by far one of your most useful tools. Get a 6-, 8-, or 10-inch knife, depending on your comfort level. Seriously, a huge knife does you no good if you're nervous holding it. Go to the store and pretend to chop. I prefer thinner blades for precision, but it's such a personal choice.

PARING KNIFE

I recommend having a straight-edge paring knife as well as a serrated one. The serrated edge is nice for small projects, like cutting cherry tomatoes or small citrus fruits.

SMALL TOOLS

BOX GRATER

This is easily one of my most prized tools. Get a utilitarian-style one made of steel. It'll last forever.

BRUSHES

Get a classic pastry brush, which is basically a 1½-inch-wide paintbrush, or a small silicone version. Both work well.

FINE RASP GRATER

The most famous brand is Microplane. They are great, but other brands work well, too, whether you're zesting citrus or dealing with small garlic cloves.

FISH PLIERS

Okay, don't look for fish pliers. Instead, go to the hardware store and pick up needle-nose pliers. They are all you need for removing pin bones when the fishmonger forgets. (Store them in the kitchen so you don't accidentally use them for non-food-related projects.)

FISH SPATULA

These are sometimes called offset slotted spatulas and have an especially thin, flexible metal blade. This is the only spatula I have (except a giant one I use for grilling) and I use it for everything: cooking and transferring delicate fish fillets, serving vegetables, moving cookies to a cooling rack . . .

ICE CREAM SCOOPS

Not just for ice cream. You can use them for scooping cookies, meatballs, and even chocolate truffles. Get ones with a mechanical release for even portioning. You should buy 1-, 1½-, and 2-tablespoon scoops if you can.

INSTANT-READ OR PROBE THERMOMETER

I don't care how experienced you might be in the kitchen—a digital thermometer is your best friend. Even after years of cooking, I still rely on mine. Why? It takes away the need to guess. I love Taylor brand thermometers because their compact pen-style thermometer comes in a waterproof version.

MEASURING CUPS

You should *always* measure liquids in a liquid measuring cup and dry ingredients in dry measuring cups. OXO and Pyrex both make great liquid measuring cups. As for dry, look for ones that nest so they are easy to store.

OFFSET SPATULA

These allow you to spread frostings and other foods evenly. Like many tools, you should keep small and large versions on hand.

RUBBER SPATULAS

Always stick with silicone ones. I like to keep two on hand: a long, skinny one that can fit through the opening of a jar and a full-size one for folding ingredients together.

SCISSORS

Also known as kitchen shears. Buy sturdy ones that come apart for cleaning. Wüsthof makes amazing ones.

TONGS

I like to buy large—but not too large—locking tongs with silicone tips that won't scratch nonstick skillets but can withstand the heat of my grill.

WHISKS

You should have two: small and large. The small one is great for salad dressings and sauces while the large one is nice for beating eggs and heavy cream.

THE WISDOM OF
BASICS

I have way too many friends who rely on Google for the most basic cooking questions you can imagine. Hopefully this section will get them off their computers by offering best practices for preparing everyday foods. Plus, I've shared cooking temperatures for the usual suspects—chicken, beef, and pork—as well as some handy measurements.

EASIEST CRISP BACON

The secret is (wait for it . . .) the oven. Preheat it to 400°F and line a large rimmed baking sheet with heavy-duty foil. Arrange bacon slices in a single layer and bake for 15 to 20 minutes, until browned and crisp. Using tongs, transfer the bacon to paper towels to drain and crisp more.

MISTAKE-PROOF EGGS

HARD-BOILED EGGS

Use a saucepan just big enough to hold your eggs, which will help control how quickly the water comes to a boil. Cover the eggs with water and bring to a boil, then simmer over medium-high heat for 8 minutes. Drain and cool the eggs under cold running water or in a bowl of ice water.

SOFT-BOILED EGGS

These are eggs with firm whites but runny yolks, delicious warm or cold (see page 45). Fill a medium bowl with ice and water to make an ice bath. Fill a medium saucepan halfway with water and bring to a boil over high heat. Using a slotted spoon, carefully lower the eggs into the water and simmer over medium heat for exactly 7 minutes. Using the slotted spoon, transfer the eggs to the ice bath to cool. Very gently crack the eggs on a work surface and then carefully peel off the shells.

SUNNY-SIDE UP

Fry an egg over high heat and you'll end up with unpleasantly chewy whites and dry, crumbly yolks. Instead, warm 1 to 2 tablespoons of fat (oil or butter) in a large nonstick skillet over medium heat. One at a time, crack the eggshell on a flat surface and drop the egg into the skillet, then immediately reduce the heat to low and cook sunny-side (yolk) up until the whites are firm and the yolks runny, about 5 minutes. Transfer to a plate and season with salt and pepper.

POACHED EGGS

I have a love affair with poached eggs. Read about my favorite method for cooking them on page 63.

DIY SHRIMP

SHELLING AND DEVEINING

You can usually buy pre-cleaned shrimp, but you should definitely learn how to clean them yourself because you never know when you might have to. Plus, it's easy! Start by peeling off the shell. Whether you choose to leave the tail intact or not is up to you. Using a paring knife, score the shrimp lengthwise along the back to reveal the vein. Lay the shrimp flat on a paper towel, then scrape out the vein.

REMOVING THE VEIN BUT NOT THE SHELL

This is ideal if you're making peel-and-eat shrimp (see page 191), or if you want to grill the shrimp shell-on (this keeps 'em juicier). Using the tip of a scissors blade, cut along the back of the shrimp through the shell, leaving it otherwise intact. Using a paring knife, remove and discard the vein. Fold the shell back around the shrimp. Done!

FLUFFIEST WHITE RICE

I can't even tell you how many people ask me how to steam white rice. Start by rinsing your rice well, until the water runs clear. This will help ensure the grains don't clump (if you want your rice sticky, don't rinse it). For every 1 cup dry rice, use 1½ cups water. In a medium saucepan, bring the water to a boil over high heat. Add the rice and a generous pinch of salt, but don't stir it yet. Return the water to a boil, and then stir it once, cover, and simmer over low heat until all the water has been absorbed and the rice is tender, about 20 minutes for 1 to 2 cups rice. Turn off the heat and let it steam, covered, for 20 minutes, then fluff it up with a fork.

BEST-EVER QUINOA

My friend Kay Chun taught me this spectacular way to cook quinoa, and I've used it ever since. First, rinse your quinoa as it's coated in naturally occurring compounds called saponins, which can make it taste bitter. Plus, quinoa can get a bit dusty. Next, fill a medium saucepan with water, bring it to a boil, and add a generous pinch of salt. Add the quinoa and simmer over medium-high heat until tender, about 10 minutes. Drain it well in a fine sieve, shaking out any excess water. Return the quinoa to the hot saucepan, cover, and let it steam for 10 minutes. Fluff it with a fork and serve, or spread on a large baking sheet to cool and use later.

PERFECTLY COOKED MEAT

Keep an instant-read or probe thermometer handy and use the following temperature guides.

CHICKEN

BREAST: 160°F
(taken from the thickest part)

DARK MEAT: 165°F
(taken from the inner thigh or drumstick nearest the bone)

Pull the beef from the pan, grill, or oven at the appropriate temperature and then let it rest, uncovered, for 10 to 15 minutes before serving.

RARE: 115°F

MEDIUM RARE: 120 to 125°F

MEDIUM: 135 to 140°F

MEDIUM WELL: I do not recommend this, but the temp is 150°F

WELL DONE: No, please, don't!

Too many people want their pork well done. I completely disagree, as would just about any chef. Always take the temperature from the thickest part of the meat. For chops and tenderloin, let them rest, as you would beef.

TENDERLOIN: 135°F

BONELESS CHOPS: 135°F

BONE-IN CHOPS: 135 to 140°F

GROUND PORK: 160 to 165°F

ALL-PURPOSE
CONVERSION CHART

Pinch	=	⅛ teaspoon		
1 tablespoon	=	3 teaspoons	=	½ ounce
⅛ cup	=	2 tablespoons	=	1 ounce
¼ cup	=	4 tablespoons	=	2 ounces
⅓ cup	=	5 tablespoons plus 1 teaspoon	=	barely over 2½ ounces
½ cup	=	8 tablespoons	=	4 ounces
⅔ cup	=	10 tablespoons plus 2 teaspoons	=	almost 5¼ ounces
¾ cup	=	12 tablespoons	=	6 ounces
1 cup	=	16 tablespoons	=	8 ounces
1 pint	=	2 cups	=	16 ounces
1 quart	=	4 cups	=	32 ounces
1 gallon	=	4 quarts	=	128 ounces

PARTY FOODS & SNACKS

IS THERE ANYTHING MORE STRESSFUL than falling behind on your party prep, knowing your guests are en route and your doorbell could ring any second? Okay, maybe there are more stressful things, but if you entertain as much as I do then you totally get my point. In the midst of all the last-minute craziness—tidying up, fluffing pillows, lighting candles, updating your playlist—tackling a complicated recipe is a guaranteed party fail. Instead, what you serve should be simple, smart, and, most important, make-ahead. That's why I've assembled this collection of sure-fire crowd-pleasers, starting with my biggest entertaining obsession: crudités.

Modern
CRUDITÉS

Crudités Ombrés 30
Crudités Vertes 33
Crudités Blanches 34

WHIPPED
FETA DIP
with Dried Herb Oil
36

Pickled
BEET DIP
37

ROASTED
SALSA
VERDE
39

Not-So-Classic
ONION DIP
40

BUTTER BEAN &
HEARTS OF PALM
DIP
41

LEMONY
ARTICHOKE
DIP
42

Herbed Tortilla
CRISPS
43

GARLICKY SMOKED SALMON
RILLETTES
with Rye Crisps
44

Soft-Boiled
EGGS
with Sriracha-Sesame Sauce
45

Pomegranate-Glazed
Turkish
MEATBALLS
with Salted Yogurt & Mint
46

SWEET CORN
QUESO
with Pepperoni Crumbs
49

Spicy
BEER NUTS
with Rosemary
50

TANGY BAKED CHICKEN
WINGS
51

AVOCADO PIZZA
with Dukka
52

Smoked Trout, Beet &
Radish Matzo
TARTINES
55

PORK
SHUMAI
with Vinegar–Soy Sauce
56

MODERN CRUDITÉS

SERVES 4
(PER POUND OF
VEGETABLES)

For me, fresh and crunchy crudités are a party essential, whether I've invited four friends for dinner or forty for a raucous holiday blowout. Not only do platters of raw veggies prevent guests from filling up before the meal, they bring something beautiful and interactive to the table. The secret to elevating the experience is combining a variety of flavors and textures. Plus, I think it is quite chic to make a crudités platter with a bunch of veggies that are all the same hue. It might sound a little fussy but try it: Your unsuspecting guests will be stunned. Set it out with one or more dips (all of which you can make days in advance) and that's really all you need to get the party started. And with every compliment you can say, "Oh, you like it? It's no big deal—I just cut up whatever I had in the crisper drawer."

RECIPE CONTINUES

CRUDITÉS OMBRÉS

Ombré cakes were kind of a big deal last year on Pinterest, and I predict crudités ombrés will be next. Ombré is a gradual blending of one color hue into another, typically on a spectrum from lighter to darker. Here, I've picked vegetables that range from deep purple to pink to white.

NO. 1
PURPLE CARROTS

Buy the smallest carrots you can find, scrub them, and serve them whole or halved. If you can only find medium to large ones, cut them lengthwise into two or three spears. For maximum visual effect, arrange the pieces with the purple side out.

NO. 2
RADICCHIO

The bitterness of radicchio makes it great for dunking into something sweet, like my creamy beet dip (page 37), but it's also terrific with my hearts of palm dip (page 41). If using radicchio from Treviso, just pull the leaves off as you would for Belgian endive and Little Gem lettuce. If using traditional radicchio, cut the whole head in half through the core and then cut each half into very thin wedges.

NO. 3
BREAKFAST RADISHES

For a little drama, cut these to look like flowers. (Nope, it's not some special trick I learned from a Japanese vegetable carver!) Using a paring knife, make a lengthwise cut through a radish about halfway from the top. Rotate it 90 degrees and repeat, almost like marking an "X." After a 30-minute soak in ice water the radish will curl outward into "petals."

NO. 4
EASTER RADISHES

These range from light purple to white. Place the white ones near the Japanese turnips. Use the remaining ones to build a nice transition from purples to pinks. Serve the smaller radishes whole. If they're large, cut them in half lengthwise. If you have time, soak the radishes in a big bowl of water for about 20 minutes to make them terrifically crisp and keep them from drying out.

NO. 5
CHIOGGIA BEETS

Not everyone is into eating raw beets, but I happen to love the earthy flavor of Chioggia beets. I also adore their white and pink spirals. If the beets are small, just give them a good scrub and then either cut them into super-thin wedges or rounds, or shave them with a mandoline. If they're bigger and have thicker skins, you might want to peel them first.

NO. 6
NINJA RADISHES

These medium-size radishes are oblong with a pale purple skin. They're purple and white on the inside, which makes them absolutely perfect for a cruidités ombrés platter. Because they tend to be firmer than most radishes, I prefer to cut them into thin slices.

NO. 7
FENNEL

Some people love fennel and others love to hate it. Personally, I adore the licorice-y flavor it brings to a crudité platter. The easiest way to prepare it is to first take off the fibrous outer parts, then cut the bulb in half lengthwise. Hold the bulb with the cut side up so you can see the core, then cut it into thin wedges (the core holds the wedges together).

NO. 8
JAPANESE TURNIPS

See page 34.

CRUDITÉS OMBRÉS

CRUDITÉS VERTES
PAGE 33

CRUDITÉS VERTES

Pile these beautiful green veggies on a big platter and serve them alongside any of the dips from this chapter. These are especially wonderful with my lemony whipped feta (page 36).

NO. 9
BROCCOLINI

I love using broccoli for crudités, but the smaller florets and long, thin stalks of Broccolini feel new and exciting. I trim the very ends of the stalks and then shave off the thickest skin with a vegetable peeler. You can leave the Broccolini spears whole, but I prefer to cut them in half lengthwise (or in thirds if they're huge). This makes them more manageable to eat and also multiplies the number of people they serve.

NO. 10
SUGAR SNAP PEAS

Who doesn't love eating these raw, especially in the summer when they're so sweet? All you have to do is remove the top strings. To make it easy, I pinch the very tip of each pea and drag it lengthwise. You can pull off the bottom strings, too, if you find them annoying to eat (I don't).

NO. 11
PERSIAN CUCUMBERS

These are a little like kirby cukes, the kind often used for pickles, but I think they're just right for crudités because they have a crisp, thin skin and can be cut into irregular spears that make a platter look delightfully rustic (perfect shapes are so passé). Just use my neat cutting technique to get those pretty pieces: Slice the cucumber on an extreme angle, then roll it 90 degrees and make another angled cut. Keep rolling and cutting until you're done.

NO. 12
ROMANESCO

Romanesco is related to cauliflower, but it's emerald green and spiky, mild in flavor, and super crunchy. To prep it for the platter, hold it in a large bowl with the florets facing down. Using a knife, cut off the florets, rotating the head as you cut and letting the pieces fall into the bowl.

NO. 13
LITTLE GEM LETTUCE

I've started seeing this variety of lettuce at restaurants and grocery stores everywhere, and now I'm a believer, too. The leaves are reminiscent of the very inner part of romaine but are more compact, with a sweeter flavor. They're known to be great for salads that you can eat with your hands, so why *not* serve them with dips?

NO. 14
CELERY RIBS

Ah, celery: What crudité platter is complete without it? I use the entire head, including the pale inner ribs and the dark outer ones. I like to cut them on an extreme angle into long slivers. I usually shoot for ½ inch thick but obviously perfection is not what I'm going for here. They end up looking a bit like half-moons that have been stretched into exaggerated ovals.

NO. 15
BELGIAN ENDIVE

The juicy, crisp texture combined with the nutty-sweet flavor and natural cup shape make these spears a crudité must. Plus, Belgian endive practically preps itself! Just slide your pointer finger between each leaf and the core and snap at the base. Try not to break the leaves, though, because they will go brown pretty quickly.

CRUDITÉS BLANCHES

White vegetables, arranged thoughtfully on a platter, make for one heck of an elegant presentation. Put them on a dark—even black—plate and they become strikingly modern. Most of the vegetables here can be found year-round, but feel free to substitute anything that's in season. I prefer these with my pickled beet dip (page 37) but they're also awesome with my whipped feta (page 36).

NO. 16
DAIKON

Crisp and mild, daikon is one of my favorite radishes. It's often used for kimchi or Korean beef braises, but I also eat it raw. Be sure to buy firm ones (bendy daikon isn't good daikon) that smell fresh. I peel them, but you don't have to. If the daikon is huge, cut it in half lengthwise and then cut it crosswise into ¼-inch-thick half-moons. If it's small, it will look pretty cut into rounds. Radishes often dry out easily, so soak the sliced daikon in ice water for about 15 minutes before serving.

NO. 17
CAULIFLOWER

Lately, I've noticed a lot of people blanching cauliflower, but I much prefer it raw. Cut the head into florets, like you would broccoli, or just break it up with your hands. When I have time, I season the pieces by soaking them in ice water mixed with a handful of kosher salt and maybe a little vinegar. Just be sure to drain the cauliflower well before serving, or give it a whirl in a salad spinner.

NO. 18
WHITE ASPARAGUS

I don't love the harsh flavor or coarse texture of raw asparagus, either white or green, so I always blanch them quickly even for a "raw" platter. (What's wrong with breaking the rules every now and then, huh?) To prep the asparagus, bring a large pot of salted water to a boil, and set up a big bowl of ice water nearby. Cook the asparagus for a minute or two, until crisp-tender. Using a slotted spoon or tongs, transfer to the ice bath and let cool. Drain and pat dry before serving.

NO. 19
FENNEL

Prep it just as you would for an ombré arrangement (see page 30). Or cut it into graceful slices. To do that, first divide the bulb in half lengthwise. Place the halves cut-side down on a work surface and, using a large knife, very thinly slice lengthwise into long strips. Soak the strips in ice water for about 15 minutes, until they curl ever so slightly and become impossibly crisp, then drain well.

NO. 20
BELGIAN ENDIVE

I love Belgian endive leaves on both a green and white platter of veggies. Like I said, Mother Nature made them natural scoopers of dips. And guess what? I heard a rumor that there's just one calorie per leaf.

NO. 21
JAPANESE TURNIPS

These tender and sweet turnips look a bit like perfectly shaped radishes but are milder in flavor and paler. They're tedious to peel, so don't bother. I cut the larger ones lengthwise into quarters but most are small enough to be served whole or halved. As with daikon, I like to give these a quick soak in ice water before serving so they're extra crisp and juicy.

CRUDITÉS BLANCHES

WHIPPED
FETA DIP

with Dried Herb Oil

TOTAL TIME
10 MIN

MAKES 2 CUPS

Feta undergoes a personality transformation when whipped in a food processor with olive oil and milk, becoming incredibly airy and light. The result is a dip that's delicious with any of the crudité setups here, but makes the boldest visual statement with the *blanche* (white) platter (page 34).

8 ounces feta cheese, crumbled

¼ cup extra-virgin olive oil

¼ cup whole milk

½ teaspoon finely grated lemon zest

1½ tablespoons fresh lemon juice

Freshly ground white pepper

Dried Herb Oil (page 279) or extra-virgin olive oil, for drizzling

Crudités, chips, or bread, for serving

In a food processor, combine the feta, olive oil, milk, lemon zest, and lemon juice. Puree until very smooth, about 1 minute. Season the dip with white pepper. Scrape into a shallow serving bowl. Drizzle with Dried Herb Oil or olive oil and serve with crudités, chips, or bread.

DO IT AHEAD   The whipped feta dip can be refrigerated for up to 3 days. Let stand at room temperature for 30 minutes and then stir before serving.

PICKLED
BEET DIP

HANDS-ON TIME
10 MIN

TOTAL TIME
25 MIN

MAKES 2 CUPS

Pickled beets from a can tend to get an "Ewwww!" reaction. But they have a special place in my heart because of Grandma Barbara. One day, as a once-in-a-blue-moon treat, she brought me to King's Table, a popular chain of buffet restaurants. When I scouted the salad bar I saw, piled higher than my head, a mysterious fuchsia vegetable. "What is that?" I asked Grandma. Without skipping a beat, she grabbed a pair of tongs and put some of those beets on my plate. It was love at first bite. This ultra-simple dip, with the traditional eastern European flavors of beets and horseradish, reminds me of that day.

1 (16-ounce) jar pickled beets, drained

¾ cup plain Greek yogurt or sour cream

1 tablespoon freshly grated or prepared horseradish

1 garlic clove, crushed

Kosher salt and freshly ground black pepper

Snipped fresh dill, for topping

Crudités, chips, or pita chips, for serving

In a food processor, combine the beets, yogurt, horseradish, and garlic and puree until very smooth; scrape down the sides of the bowl a few times while pureeing. Scrape the dip into a medium bowl and season with salt and pepper. Cover and refrigerate until chilled, about 15 minutes. Top with snipped dill and serve with crudités, chips, or pita chips.

DO IT AHEAD   The beet dip can be refrigerated in an airtight container for up to 1 week. Top with snipped dill just before serving.

WHIPPED FETA DIP

with Dried Herb Oil

PAGE 36

ROASTED
SALSA VERDE

HANDS-ON TIME
15 MIN

TOTAL TIME
45 MIN PLUS
COOLING

MAKES 3 CUPS

I know what you're thinking: "Is this even a dip? Isn't it really more of a sauce?" You know, I try not to get caught up in this kind of negative thinking, though I will reveal that later in the book I pour this salsa verde all over my enchiladas (page 208). Bottom line, any vegetable is going to taste better when eaten with this tangy, spicy bowl of green deliciousness. So go ahead and dip already.

2   pounds tomatillos,
    husked, rinsed, and
    quartered

1   small white onion,
    coarsely chopped

2   jalapeños, quartered and
    seeded

4   garlic cloves, crushed

¼   cup extra-virgin olive oil

    Kosher salt and freshly
    ground black pepper

1   cup lightly packed fresh
    cilantro

    Crudités and tortilla
    chips, or pita chips, for
    serving

Preheat the oven to 425°F.

On a large rimmed baking sheet, toss the tomatillos, onion, jalapeños, garlic, and olive oil. Season with salt and pepper and toss again. Roast for about 30 minutes, until the tomatillos and onion are tender. Let cool, then scrape the mixture (along with any of the delicious juices from the baking sheet) into a blender or food processor. Add the cilantro and puree until nearly smooth. Season with salt and pepper. Serve right away with crudités, chips, or pita chips or refrigerate until ready to use.

DO IT AHEAD   The salsa verde can be refrigerated in an airtight container for up to 1 week.

NOT-SO-CLASSIC ONION DIP

HANDS-ON TIME
40 MIN

TOTAL TIME
2 HRS

MAKES 3 CUPS

French onion soup mix combined with sour cream: Honestly, who doesn't love it? My family served it at just about every gathering, and to nobody's surprise, it was always one of the first foods to disappear. I continued to serve the dip at parties well into my adulthood . . . until, at a summer barbecue, my friend Jeff asked for the recipe. After avoiding his gaze for nearly 15 minutes, I knew I had to come clean. But I also knew it was time to come up with a homemade version that would satisfy that nostalgic craving. Here's the result, and I'm quite happy with it.

1 cup canola oil

4 large shallots (4 ounces), thinly sliced and separated into rings

Kosher salt

1 medium yellow onion, finely chopped

1 medium red onion, finely chopped

1 (16-ounce) container sour cream

1 tablespoon garlic powder

1 tablespoon onion powder

Potato chips and crudités, for serving

Line a baking sheet with paper towels. In a large skillet, heat the oil over medium-high heat until shimmering. Add half the shallots and fry, stirring frequently, until browned and crisp, 3 to 5 minutes. Using a slotted spoon, transfer the fried shallots to the paper towels and sprinkle lightly with salt. Repeat with the remaining shallots.

Pour off all but 3 tablespoons of the oil from the skillet. Add the yellow and red onions and a generous pinch of salt. Cook over medium-high heat, stirring occasionally, until just softened, about 5 minutes. Reduce the heat to medium-low and cook, stirring occasionally, until very soft and caramelized, about 30 minutes. Let cool.

In a large bowl, mix the caramelized onions, sour cream, garlic powder, and onion powder. Reserve ¼ cup of the fried shallots for garnish. Crush the remaining shallots and stir them into the dip. Cover and refrigerate for 1 hour, stirring occasionally. Season the dip with salt and pepper. Garnish with the reserved fried shallots and serve with potato chips and crudités.

DO IT AHEAD The dip can be refrigerated in an airtight container for up to 3 days; store the reserved fried shallots at room temperature in a separate airtight container. Stir well and garnish with the reserved shallots before serving.

BUTTER BEAN & HEARTS OF PALM DIP

HANDS-ON TIME
30 MIN

TOTAL TIME
1 HR 15 MIN

MAKES
2½ CUPS

This recipe relies on one of my secret weapons for healthy cooking: canned hearts of palm, the inner core of palm trees. Resembling thick little white batons, they're naturally low in calories, with a mild, slightly nutty flavor reminiscent of artichokes. *Zhoozh* them in a blender with butter beans (aka lima beans) for a light and lush puree that practically demands a raw veggie stick.

1 (14-ounce) can butter beans, drained and rinsed

1 (14-ounce) can hearts of palm, drained

2 tablespoons fresh lemon juice

2 tablespoons extra-virgin olive oil

2 garlic cloves, finely grated

Kosher salt and freshly ground black pepper

Crudités or pita chips, for serving

In a food processor or blender, combine the butter beans, hearts of palm, lemon juice, olive oil, and garlic and puree until very smooth. Scrape into a small serving bowl and season generously with salt and pepper. Cover with plastic wrap and refrigerate until well chilled, about 1 hour. Serve with crudités or pita chips.

DO IT AHEAD The dip can be refrigerated in an airtight container for up to 3 days.

LEMONY
ARTICHOKE DIP

HANDS-ON TIME
15 MIN

TOTAL TIME
30 MIN

SERVES 6 TO 8

When I was growing up in California, artichokes were an everyday kind of food. During high school, I'd drive across town to my favorite lunch spot, Manny's California Fresh, for whole steamed 'chokes that I'd dip, leaf by leaf, in butter and vinegar, then scrape between my teeth. That nutty, starchy flavor was heaven to me.

Eventually, I turned to online cooking videos to learn how to "butcher" raw artichokes so I could cook the prickly little beasts at home. It takes patience, confidence, and care to get to the good stuff—the heart. But boy, did I want the good stuff. I would spend a full hour just cutting out enough hearts for a single batch of my favorite diner-style artichoke dip. At some point I just gave up. Artichokes 1, Justin 0.

But then, one great day, I discovered frozen artichoke hearts. (Hear me out.) These are no ordinary ho-hum frozen vegetable. They're so easy to use, and so full of pure flavor. Seriously, all they need is a little bit of chopping and then it's go time.

½ cup mayonnaise

1 teaspoon finely grated lemon zest

2 tablespoons fresh lemon juice

1 garlic clove, finely grated

2 dashes of Tabasco or other Louisiana-style hot sauce

2 (9-ounce) packages frozen artichoke heart quarters, thawed, patted dry, and coarsely chopped

1½ cups shredded Monterey Jack cheese

¼ cup chopped fresh chives, plus more for sprinkling

Kosher salt and freshly ground black pepper

½ cup panko bread crumbs

2 tablespoons unsalted butter, melted

Herbed Tortilla Crisps (recipe follows) or pita chips, for serving

Preheat the oven to 400°F.

In a large bowl, whisk together the mayonnaise, lemon zest, lemon juice, garlic, and Tabasco. Fold in the artichoke hearts, cheese, and chives. Season the dip with salt and pepper and scrape into a 1-quart glass or ceramic baking dish.

In a small bowl, toss the panko with the melted butter and a pinch each of salt and pepper. Sprinkle the panko evenly on top of the dip. Bake for about 15 minutes, until the dip is hot and the topping is golden. Sprinkle with chopped chives and serve with Herbed Tortilla Crisps or pita chips.

DO IT AHEAD The unbaked dip can be refrigerated overnight. Let stand at room temperature for 15 minutes before baking and garnishing with chives.

HERBED
TORTILLA CRISPS

TOTAL TIME
15 MIN

SERVES 6

I'll let you in on a little secret: these crisps were the result of a happy accident. I invited some friends over for an impromptu feast of grilled fish tacos and endless margaritas. This was the perfect meal for a last-minute get-together because all I needed to do was grill the fish and prep a few tasty accompaniments, like shredded cabbage, lime wedges, and warm tortillas. I had everything on the table except the tortillas so I threw a few on the grill, then popped back into the kitchen to refill my margarita. Big mistake. After just a minute on the grill, the tortillas burned on the edges and got so crisp we ended up eating our fish on tostadas. It all worked out okay because our fish tostadas were delicious and, more importantly, I discovered a new technique for homemade tortilla crisps.

6   (6- to-8-inch) flour
    tortillas

    Extra-virgin olive oil, for
    brushing

    Paprika

    Dried oregano

    Dried thyme

    Kosher salt and freshly
    ground black pepper

Light a grill or preheat a grill pan.

In batches, brush the tortillas with olive oil and sprinkle with paprika, oregano, and thyme, then season with salt and pepper. Grill over medium-high heat, turning once or twice, until lightly browned and crisp, about 1 minute total. Let cool, then break into shards and serve.

DO IT AHEAD   The cooled tortilla chips can be stored in an airtight container at room temperature overnight.

GARLICKY SMOKED SALMON
RILLETTES

with Rye Crisps

HANDS-ON TIME
20 MIN

TOTAL TIME
1 HR 30 MIN

MAKES 1 CUP

My husband, Jason, was totally weirded out the first time I served him this recipe. I described it as "salmon spread," to which he replied, "Salmon shouldn't be spreadable!" That's why I decided to use the term *rillettes*, which generally refers to a rustic pâté made with pork. I opt for smoked salmon instead of fresh because it's insanely easy to use and offers so much concentrated flavor. PS: Jason loves it.

2 tablespoons unsalted butter

1 large shallot, minced

2 large garlic cloves, minced

¾ teaspoon caraway seeds

Kosher salt

4 ounces smoked salmon, finely chopped

⅓ cup sour cream

2 tablespoons minced fresh chives, plus more for sprinkling

¼ teaspoon finely grated lemon zest

1 tablespoon fresh lemon juice

Freshly ground black pepper

Rye crisps, such as Wasa, for serving

In a small skillet, melt the butter over medium heat. Add the shallot, garlic, caraway, and a generous pinch of salt. Cook, stirring, until the shallot is softened and just starting to brown, about 5 minutes. Scrape into a medium bowl and let cool slightly, then stir in the salmon, sour cream, chives, lemon zest, and lemon juice. Season the rillettes with salt and pepper.

Spoon the rillettes into an 8-ounce glass jar with a tight-fitting lid (this is what I do, but any container with a lid will work just fine) and refrigerate for at least 1 hour. Let the rillettes stand at room temperature for 10 to 15 minutes before serving on rye crisps, sprinkled with minced chives.

DO IT AHEAD   The rillettes can be refrigerated for up to 3 days.

SOFT-BOILED
EGGS
with Sriracha-Sesame Sauce

HANDS-ON TIME
15 MIN

TOTAL TIME
25 MIN

SERVES 6

I moved to Manhattan in 2014, to a downtown neighborhood known as the Financial District. Although the area is becoming more residential, with more good places to eat, it's still a bit of a wasteland at night after the bankers go home. So thank heaven for the North End Grill. The chef, Eric Korsch, serves an egg-mayonnaise starter that I just adore: boiled eggs on baby lettuces, topped with housemade mayonnaise. I mean, what's not to like? Okay, maybe this recipe's kinda old-fashioned, but I think it deserves a comeback. I'll do my part with an Asian-inflected riff. I not only serve these eggs at parties but sometimes make a few at breakfast, just for me.

6 large eggs

½ cup mayonnaise

1 tablespoon sriracha

1 teaspoon toasted sesame oil

Kosher salt

Toasted sesame seeds, for sprinkling

Minced fresh chives or scallions, for sprinkling

Fill a medium bowl with ice and water to make an ice bath. Fill a medium saucepan halfway with water and bring to a boil over high heat. Using a slotted spoon, carefully lower the eggs into the water and simmer over medium heat for exactly 7 minutes. Using the slotted spoon, transfer the eggs to the ice bath to cool completely.

Meanwhile, in a small bowl, whisk together the mayonnaise, sriracha, and sesame oil. Season the sauce with salt.

Very gently crack the eggs on a work surface and then carefully peel off the shells. Using a paring knife, cut the eggs in half lengthwise and transfer the halves to a small platter (be careful not to hold the cut eggs sideways for more than a second or you'll lose all that delicious yolk). Spoon a little bit of the sauce on each egg and sprinkle them with toasted sesame seeds and minced chives or scallions. Serve cold or at room temperature.

DO IT AHEAD The soft-boiled eggs and sauce can be refrigerated in separate airtight containers for up to 2 days.

TIP One thing that can be annoying with serving eggs like these (deviled eggs, too), is that they easily slide all over the place. I recommend sprinkling a thin layer of kosher salt on the platter, or just under each egg, so the food stays put.

POMEGRANATE-GLAZED
TURKISH MEATBALLS
with Salted Yogurt & Mint

TOTAL TIME
45 MIN

SERVES 6

Not all meatballs need to be the Italian-American kind, packed with cheese and drowning in tomato sauce. The ones here are inspired by *kofte*, the small, oval-shaped Turkish patties filled with grated onion, garlic, and spices. They're easy to make, with a relatively short list of ingredients, and best of all, they're tender and juicy, with a tangy pomegranate juice glaze that boosts their lovability even more. What's the secret? Ground lamb, which tends to be just a little fattier than ground beef or pork. Trust me, you'll happily make this recipe on the regular when you realize how foolproof it is.

2   slices day-old white sandwich bread or any other soft bread you have on hand

1   pound ground lamb

½   small onion, finely grated

2   garlic cloves, finely grated

1   tablespoon sweet paprika

1   teaspoon ground cumin

¾   cup finely chopped fresh mint, plus more for sprinkling

Kosher salt and freshly ground black pepper

1   tablespoon canola oil

2   cups no-sugar-added pomegranate juice

¼   cup pomegranate seeds

1   cup plain Greek yogurt

In a large bowl, cover the bread with ¼ cup water and let stand for 5 minutes. Add the lamb, onion, garlic, paprika, cumin, ½ cup of the mint, 2 teaspoons salt, and ½ teaspoon pepper. Knead the mixture until well blended. Using a 1-tablespoon measure, firmly scoop the mixture into 1¼-inch meatballs.

In a large skillet, heat the canola oil over medium-high heat. Add the meatballs and cook, turning, until browned all over and nearly cooked through, 6 to 8 minutes. Using a slotted spoon, transfer the meatballs to a plate.

Pour off the fat from the skillet. Add the pomegranate juice and bring to a boil over high heat, then reduce the heat to medium and simmer until reduced to the consistency of a glaze, about 10 minutes. Return the meatballs to the skillet and cook, turning the meatballs frequently, until cooked through and glazed, 3 to 5 minutes. Transfer to a platter and sprinkle with the pomegranate seeds.

In a small serving bowl, whisk together the yogurt, the remaining ¼ cup mint, and a generous pinch of salt. Sprinkle with mint and serve with the meatballs.

DO IT AHEAD   The uncooked meatballs can be refrigerated in an airtight container overnight.

SWEET CORN QUESO

with Pepperoni Crumbs

TOTAL TIME
40 MIN

SERVES 6

I have to confess, I'm crazy about the queso (Tex-Mex cheese dip) from the Chili's restaurant chain. Growing up, I'd go every week with my friend Maggie and we'd order enchilada soup and a salad with just vinegar and oil on the side. But every now and then, we'd splurge on the queso, which came with all the tortilla chips we could eat. My homemade version is quite a bit healthier, even with those awesome pepperoni crumbs.

Pepperoni Crumbs

- 2 ounces thinly sliced pepperoni, chopped
- ½ cup panko bread crumbs
- Kosher salt
- 1 tablespoon extra-virgin olive oil

Queso

- 2 tablespoons unsalted butter
- 2 tablespoons extra-virgin olive oil
- 2 cups fresh (from 4 ears) or thawed frozen corn kernels
- 1 small red onion, finely chopped
- 1 jalapeño, seeded and minced, plus thinly sliced jalapeño for garnish
- 2 garlic cloves, minced
- Kosher salt and freshly ground black pepper
- 1 tablespoon cornstarch
- 8 ounces Monterey Jack cheese, shredded (2 cups)
- Chopped fresh cilantro, for sprinkling
- Tortilla chips, for serving

Make the crumbs In a food processor, pulse the pepperoni until finely chopped. Add the panko and a pinch of salt and pulse until fine crumbs form. Scrape into a large cast-iron skillet. Add the olive oil and cook over medium heat, stirring until crisp, about 5 minutes. Scrape onto a plate and let cool. Wipe out the skillet.

Make the queso In the same skillet, melt the butter in the olive oil over medium heat. Add the corn, red onion, jalapeño, garlic, and a pinch each of salt and pepper. Cook, stirring until the vegetables are tender, about 10 minutes. Add 1½ cups water and bring to a boil over medium-high heat. Stir in the cornstarch until incorporated, then simmer until thickened, about 3 minutes. Stir in the cheese until melted. Season the queso with salt and pepper.

Scatter the pepperoni crumbs on top, then sprinkle with thinly sliced jalapeño and chopped cilantro. Serve hot with tortilla chips.

SPICY BEER NUTS

with Rosemary

HANDS-ON TIME
5 MIN

TOTAL TIME
35 MIN

MAKES 2 CUPS

This is the ultimate five-minute snack that will have your guests searching every bowl in your house for more. My sneaky little shortcut is buying a big can of mixed roasted nuts and then quickly toasting them in a skillet with olive oil, rosemary (which gets nicely crunchy), red pepper flakes, sugar, and garlic powder. Small effort, big reward. Try it at your next cocktail party or heck, even Game Day.

¼ cup extra-virgin olive oil

¼ cup fresh rosemary leaves

2 cups mixed roasted nuts

1 teaspoon red pepper flakes

1 teaspoon sugar

½ teaspoon garlic powder

Kosher salt

In a large skillet, heat the olive oil over medium-high heat. Add the rosemary and cook, stirring, until the sizzling slows, about 30 seconds. Add the nuts, red pepper flakes, sugar, garlic powder, and a generous pinch of salt. Cook, tossing, until the nuts are very fragrant, 3 to 5 minutes. Transfer to a large plate to cool. Serve warm or at room temperature.

DO IT AHEAD   The nuts can be stored in an airtight container at room temperature for up to 3 days. You can warm them in the oven for a couple of minutes before serving, if you like.

TANGY BAKED CHICKEN WINGS

HANDS-ON TIME
15 MIN

TOTAL TIME
55 MIN

SERVES 2 TO 4

People go to bars to eat Buffalo chicken wings; no one really makes them at home. C'mon, who likes to fry? But I sometimes re-create the dish by baking wings until super crisp, then tossing them in hot sauce or my BBQ Sauce Vinaigrette. The dressing is just thick enough to coat the wings without being gloppy, though you'll still need to keep some napkins on hand—these are messy!

3 pounds chicken wingettes and drumettes

¼ cup extra-virgin olive oil

Kosher salt and freshly ground black pepper

½ cup BBQ Sauce Vinaigrette (page 269)

¼ cup Buffalo sauce, such as Frank's RedHot

3 tablespoons unsalted butter

Preheat the oven to 450°F. Line a large rimmed baking sheet with foil.

On the baking sheet, toss the wings with the olive oil and season generously with salt and pepper. Spread in an even layer and roast for about 45 minutes, turning once or twice, until cooked through and crispy.

Meanwhile, in a small saucepan, combine the BBQ Sauce Vinaigrette, Buffalo sauce, and butter. Cook over medium-low heat, whisking, until smooth and hot, about 5 minutes.

Transfer the wings to a very large bowl, add half the sauce, and toss to coat. Serve with the remaining sauce on the side for dipping.

AVOCADO PIZZA

with Dukka

HANDS-ON TIME
15 MIN

TOTAL TIME
30 MIN

SERVES 8 AS A
STARTER

I wouldn't be the good California boy I am if I didn't use avocado in as many recipes as possible. (You know you love it too.) If I were a jokester, I'd say this pizza is almost as if all the avocado-toast pictures on your 2017 Instagram feed joined forces. This dish is essentially a puffed, golden crust that you pull out of the oven, pile with cool, tangy guacamole, and shower with homemade dukka (page 280), an Egyptian mix of toasted nuts, seeds, and spices. Store-bought pizza dough makes this recipe quick, but if you're still squeezed for time, skip the dukka and just sprinkle on toasted sesame seeds.

Extra-virgin olive oil, for greasing and drizzling

1 pound store-bought pizza dough

4 Hass avocados, halved and pitted

3 tablespoons fresh lemon juice

½ cup chopped fresh cilantro, plus more for sprinkling

Kosher salt and freshly ground black pepper

Pistachio-Almond Dukka (page 280) or toasted white and black sesame seeds, for sprinkling

Preheat the oven to 450°F. Lightly grease a large baking sheet with olive oil.

On the baking sheet, gently stretch and pull the pizza dough to form a 14-inch oval. Bake for about 15 minutes, until puffed and browned.

Meanwhile, squeeze the avocado flesh out of the skins into a medium bowl. Add the lemon juice and, using a fork or spoon, lightly mash to form a chunky paste. Stir in the cilantro and season generously with salt and pepper.

Spread the mashed avocado on the hot pizza crust. Drizzle with olive oil and sprinkle with cilantro and dukka or toasted sesame seeds. Season with salt and pepper, cut into pieces, and serve.

DO IT AHEAD The avocado mixture can be refrigerated in an airtight container overnight. To prevent the mixture from oxidizing, press a piece of plastic wrap directly onto the surface. Let stand at room temperature for 15 minutes before using on the hot pizza crust.

SMOKED TROUT, BEET & RADISH MATZO TARTINES

TOTAL TIME
15 MIN

SERVES 4

No, I did not grow up with matzo, the crackerlike Jewish bread eaten on Passover. But now, thanks to Jason, who is famous for his matzo brei (a kind of eggy scramble), I always keep a box of the stuff in my pantry for cooking experiments. Sometimes I go sweet, covering the matzo with melted chocolate, chopped nuts, and dried fruit; sometimes I go savory, crushing it into bits to make bread crumbs. Here I use matzo as the base for an open-face sandwich, spread with chive mayo and topped with two completely underappreciated supermarket ingredients: smoked trout and packaged steamed beets.

½ cup mayonnaise or plain Greek yogurt

2 tablespoons fresh lemon juice

2 tablespoons finely chopped fresh chives, plus snipped chives for sprinkling

1 tablespoon finely grated fresh horseradish or drained prepared horseradish

Kosher salt and freshly ground black pepper

2 pieces of matzo

1 (8-ounce) package smoked trout, skin and bones discarded, flesh flaked

4 small steamed beets (from one 6- to 8-ounce package), thinly sliced

4 radishes, thinly sliced

In a small bowl, whisk together the mayonnaise, lemon juice, chives, and horseradish. Season the mayonnaise with salt and pepper.

Spread the mayonnaise on the matzo and arrange the trout, beets, and radishes on top. Sprinkle with snipped chives and season with salt and pepper. Break the matzo into pieces and serve.

VARIATION Instead of smoked trout, use a can of tuna or sardines in olive oil. Just drain off the oil and break the fish into chunks.

PORK SHUMAI

with Vinegar–Soy Sauce

TOTAL TIME
40 MIN

MAKES 14 TO 16

If you've ever wanted to make your own Chinese dumplings but felt nervous about your folding abilities, friends, this is the recipe for you. Shumai are probably the easiest dumplings to whip up because you don't have to worry about sealing the edges: You just fold the wrapper up around the filling, leaving the top open like a little cup. Shumai look a little rustic, but I think that's what makes them so pretty. I always double the recipe so I have extra in the freezer for unexpected guests or a fast weeknight meal.

½   pound ground pork

4   scallions, minced, plus more for sprinkling

3½ tablespoons peeled and minced fresh ginger

3½ tablespoons low-sodium soy sauce

3½ tablespoons unseasoned rice vinegar

1   teaspoon toasted sesame oil

½   teaspoon kosher salt

¼   teaspoon freshly ground black pepper

    All-purpose flour, for dusting

16 round wonton wrappers

    Canola oil, for greasing

    Sambal oelek or other Asian chile sauce, for serving

In a medium bowl, mix the pork with the scallions, ginger, 1½ tablespoons of the soy sauce, 1½ tablespoons of the vinegar, ½ teaspoon of the sesame oil, the salt, and the pepper.

Lightly dust a large baking sheet with flour. Hold one wonton wrapper in your palm, keeping the rest of the wrappers covered with a damp paper towel. Place a barely rounded tablespoon of the filling in the center and fold the wrapper up around the filling, pinching the edges all around to form an open cup (it's okay if you pinch the wrapper with some of the meat; it doesn't need to be perfect). Transfer the dumpling to the baking sheet and cover with a damp paper towel. Repeat with the remaining wrappers and filling.

Fill a large saucepan with ¾ inch of water and put a metal steamer basket in the bottom. Lightly oil the steamer basket and then bring the water to a simmer. Add half the dumplings to the steamer basket, cover partially, and steam over medium-low heat until firm, about 8 minutes. Transfer to a small platter and tent with foil. Repeat with the remaining shumai.

Meanwhile, in a small bowl, whisk together the remaining 2 tablespoons soy sauce, 2 tablespoons vinegar, and ½ teaspoon sesame oil. Sprinkle with additional minced scallions and serve with the shumai and sambal oelek.

DO IT AHEAD   The formed uncooked shumai can be refrigerated in an airtight container overnight. Alternatively, freeze the uncooked dumplings on the floured baking sheet and when firm, transfer them to a plastic bag and freeze for up to 1 month. Don't defrost them before cooking; just cook them for a couple of minutes longer.

RECIPE CONTINUES

SHUMAI
PREP

Hold one wonton wrapper in your palm and spoon a barely rounded tablespoon of the filling in the center.

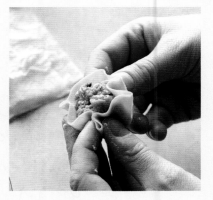

Fold the wrapper up around the filling to form an open cup.

Pinch the edges of the wrapper all around to secure the shape.

Transfer the dumpling to a baking sheet dusted with flour and cover with a damp towel.

Gently tap the dumpling on a work surface if you need to flatten the bottom.

06 21 2017

BREAKFAST, BRUNCH & OTHER EGGY THINGS

BREAKFAST, WHY DO I LOVE YOU SO? Is it because you offer an endless variety of sweet and savory combinations? Or because you're the only meal versatile enough to eat any time of day? As a kid, I adored all kinds of breakfast foods—most of all, and I mean this wholeheartedly, poached eggs on toast. That shaggy, overcooked, wet mess plopped on top of generously buttered Wonder Bread toast was pure comfort to me, and I'm not ashamed one bit.

Today, for my *Mad Genius Tips* video series, I come up with lots of crazy-smart ways to poach eggs, such as cooking a dozen at the same time in the cups of a muffin tin. But at home I more often go the traditional route. It's all good, as long as I'm bringing back the flavors of my childhood. Breakfasts and brunch in particular bring back memories of my youth, whether I'm making spicy avocado toasts topped with a poached egg or my blueberry sticky buns.

Primer:

POACHED EGGS

For the Win!

62

POACHED EGGS

& GARLICKY SPINACH

with Yogurt Hollandaise

66

Poached Eggs on Spicy

AVOCADO

Multigrain Toast

67

REUBEN TOAST

WITH POACHED EGGS

69

Poached Eggs &

WILD MUSHROOMS

on Toast

70

Mini Blueberry-Ginger

BREAKFAST BUNS

71

COCONUT-LIME

MUFFINS

72

MASA

PANCAKES

with Spiced Butter

74

GLUTEN-FREE PEPPERONI

BREAKFAST PIZZA

75

Croque Madame

HOT DISH

77

BLUEBERRY-VANILLA

BREAKFAST CEREAL

with Yogurt & Blueberry Preserves

78

Quick-Pickled

GRAPE TOMATOES

on Ricotta Toast

81

White Cheddar

FAUXFFLÉ

82

FRENCH TOAST

CASSEROLE

with Caramelized Peaches

83

PRIMER:
POACHED
EGGS FOR THE WIN!

A lot of people have questions for me about how to poach eggs. (They also want to know if my hair color is natural, but *anyway*.) Maybe it's because I talk, Tweet, and Instagram constantly about this topic. Plus, I've shared a ton of outrageous poaching methods. Here's my guide to perfect eggs every time.

LOOK FOR FRESHNESS.

The fresher the egg, the tighter and prettier it'll be when poached. The whites of older eggs tend to be looser, spreading quickly once they hit the water.

ASSEMBLE THE RIGHT TOOLS.

Use a large, deep skillet instead of a saucepan; it'll be easier to see what's happening in the poaching liquid and to move the eggs around. Break eggs into a small heatproof bowl, not directly into the skillet, since that can result in broken yolks and wispy whites. Lift the cooked eggs out with a big, thin, slotted metal spoon.

USE JUST ENOUGH WATER.

You only want the water to cover the eggs—no more. If you've got too much liquid in the pan, you'll have trouble sliding the eggs in gently and they might fall to the bottom, breaking the yolks. Plus, the less water, the easier it is to control the temperature.

ADD A LITTLE DISTILLED WHITE VINEGAR.

My grandma Barbara swore by it! And so do I. Somehow the vinegar helps any loose egg whites stay close to the yolk instead of floating around. I use a bit more than most cooks—about ¼ cup—for foolproof results. If the tangy flavor bothers you, dip the poached eggs in a bowl of clean warm water before transferring them to a plate.

COOK WITH CARE.

Fill your skillet with water and heat the water over medium heat until tiny bubbles appear on the bottom of the pan. Stir in the vinegar and a generous pinch of salt. One at a time, crack eggs into the small bowl and carefully slide them into the water. Poach them over medium heat until the whites are just firm and the yolks are runny, 3 to 5 minutes. You can check the eggs by lifting them out of the water with a slotted spoon and gently prodding the whites with your fingers. Transfer to a plate if you plan to eat them immediately.

PLAN AHEAD FOR A BRUNCH PARTY.

Believe it or not, poached eggs are easy to make a day in advance. You didn't think restaurants cooked them to order, did you? Rather than transferring the eggs from the skillet straight to the plate, slide them into a large bowl of ice water to stop the cooking. Store the eggs in the ice water in the refrigerator until you're ready to eat. To reheat, using a slotted spoon, submerge the eggs in barely simmering water for 1 minute.

HOW TO
POACH
EGGS

One at a time, crack eggs into a
small bowl and carefully slide them into
the simmering water.

Poach the eggs over medium heat
for 3 to 5 minutes.

Use a thin, slotted metal spoon
to carefully lift the eggs out of the
simmering water.

Check for doneness by gently prodding
the egg with your finger. The yolks should
be soft and the whites should be firm.

If poaching the eggs in advance, transfer them to an ice bath to cool.

POACHED EGGS & GARLICKY SPINACH

with Yogurt Hollandaise

HANDS-ON TIME
35 MIN

TOTAL TIME
35 MIN

SERVES 4

I've never been one to shy away from a classic hollandaise. That said, like many people, I go through a period each year where I want to cut back on the calories (hello, bathing-suit season!) and that's where this lighter variation comes in. Even with fat-free Greek yogurt in place of butter, the sauce thickens up nicely. I eat this sans bread but it's also lovely over wheat toast.

3 large egg yolks

½ cup nonfat plain Greek yogurt

1 tablespoon fresh lemon juice

2 teaspoons Dijon mustard

Pinch of cayenne pepper

Kosher salt and freshly ground black pepper

2 tablespoons extra-virgin olive oil

6 large garlic cloves, very thinly sliced

3 (5-ounce) packages baby spinach and kale mix

¼ cup distilled white vinegar

8 large eggs

Fill a medium saucepan with 1 inch of water and bring to a simmer over medium-low heat. In a large heatproof glass bowl, whisk together the egg yolks, yogurt, lemon juice, Dijon, and cayenne. Set the bowl on the rim of the saucepan over the simmering water and cook, stirring continuously with a rubber spatula, until the sauce is hot and just thickened, about 5 minutes. Turn off the heat and season the sauce with salt and black pepper. Keep warm, stirring occasionally.

In a large deep skillet, heat the olive oil over medium heat. Add the garlic and cook, stirring, until softened and fragrant, 2 to 3 minutes. Stir in the spinach and kale mix in large handfuls, letting each batch wilt slightly before adding more. Cook, stirring, until the greens are just wilted, 3 to 5 minutes. Season with salt and pepper, then transfer to a bowl and tent with aluminum foil to keep it warm.

Wipe out the skillet and fill it with water. Heat the water over medium heat until tiny bubbles appear on the bottom. Stir in the vinegar and a generous pinch of salt. One at a time, crack the eggs into a small bowl and very carefully slide them into the water. Poach over medium heat until the whites are just firm and the yolks are runny, 3 to 5 minutes. Using a slotted spoon, transfer the eggs to a plate.

Using tongs, transfer the greens to plates and put the eggs on top. Drizzle with the hollandaise and sprinkle with black pepper. Serve right away.

POACHED EGGS

ON SPICY AVOCADO MULTIGRAIN TOAST

TOTAL TIME
30 MIN
SERVES 4

I took avocados for granted as a kid. We ate them like they were apples because they were everywhere. My family would buy thirty at a time, at less than a dollar a pop. But after moving to New York, I was shocked to discover that just one avocado could set me back $3! So instead of eating a whole avocado for breakfast, the way I did growing up, I'd spread a half on toast to make it last longer. I became obsessed with avocado toast—way before it was trendy—and its endless variations, adding everything from smoked trout to sprouts on top. Here I'm staying close to the classic with a poached egg.

¼ cup distilled white vinegar

Kosher salt

4 large eggs

2 Hass avocados, halved and pitted

2 tablespoons fresh lime juice

2 tablespoons minced scallion

2 tablespoons finely chopped fresh cilantro, plus extra leaves for sprinkling

1 fresh hot red chile, seeded and minced

1 tablespoon extra-virgin olive oil, plus more for drizzling

Freshly ground black pepper

4 slices multigrain sandwich bread, toasted

Fill a large deep skillet with water and heat over medium heat until tiny bubbles appear on the bottom. Stir in the vinegar and a generous pinch of salt. One at a time, crack the eggs into a small bowl and very carefully slide them into the water. Poach over medium heat until the whites are just firm and the yolks are runny, 3 to 5 minutes. Using a slotted spoon, transfer the eggs to a plate.

Using a spoon, scoop the avocado flesh out of the skin into a medium bowl and coarsely mash. Stir in the lime juice, scallion, cilantro, chile, and olive oil. Season the mixture with salt and pepper.

Spoon the avocado evenly on the toasts and top with the poached eggs. Sprinkle with cilantro leaves, salt, and pepper. Drizzle with olive oil and serve.

REUBEN TOAST
with Poached Eggs

POACHED EGGS &
WILD MUSHROOMS
on Toast
PAGE 70

POACHED EGGS
on Spicy Avocado Multigrain Toast
PAGE 67

REUBEN TOAST

with Poached Eggs

HANDS-ON TIME
20 MIN

TOTAL TIME
35 MIN

SERVES 4

This is my ode to one of America's greatest sandwiches, the Reuben—corned beef, Swiss cheese, sauerkraut, and Russian or Thousand Island dressing on rye. I top my open-face version with a poached egg and a cheater's Thousand Island–style sauce that can be drizzled on as is, which is my preference, or heated gently in a small saucepan or the microwave. Even without the poached egg this is definitely a knife-and-fork toast.

½ cup mayonnaise

2 tablespoons ketchup

2 tablespoons fresh lemon juice

2 tablespoons sweet pickle relish

¼ teaspoon Worcestershire sauce

¼ teaspoon hot paprika

Kosher salt and freshly ground black pepper

4 slices seeded rye bread

¼ cup distilled white vinegar

4 large eggs

6 slices Swiss cheese, halved

½ pound thinly sliced corned beef

1 cup drained sauerkraut

Snipped fresh chives, for sprinkling

Preheat the oven to 425°F.

In a medium bowl, whisk together the mayonnaise, ketchup, lemon juice, relish, Worcestershire sauce, and paprika. Season the sauce generously with salt and pepper.

On a large baking sheet, toast the bread for about 5 minutes, until lightly browned on the bottom.

Fill a large deep skillet with water and heat over medium heat until tiny bubbles appear on the bottom. Stir in the vinegar and a generous pinch of salt. One at a time, crack the eggs into a small bowl and very carefully slide them into the water. Poach over medium heat until the whites are just firm and the yolks are runny, 3 to 5 minutes. Using a slotted spoon, transfer the eggs to a plate.

Meanwhile, top each toast with a slice of cheese, one-quarter of the corned beef, and ¼ cup of the sauerkraut. Bake for about 5 minutes more, until the cheese is just melted. Top each toast with a poached egg and drizzle with the Reuben sauce. Sprinkle with snipped chives and serve immediately.

POACHED EGGS
& WILD MUSHROOMS ON TOAST

TOTAL TIME
30 MIN

SERVES 4

It seems every chef and many home cooks have strong opinions about the best way to prep mushrooms. They might be scandalized to know that sometimes I rinse my mushrooms instead of cleaning them one by one with a towel. I just don't have the patience. So shoot me! And don't get me started on the idea that mushrooms are best when they're well browned and crispy. I like 'em tender and juicy, as in this recipe. I cook the mushrooms undisturbed in a covered skillet, a technique I learned from my friend Marcia Kiesel, who worked with me for many years at *Food & Wine*. It sounds bizarre, but it's genius. At first the mushrooms steam in their own liquid; then, as the moisture evaporates, they brown and crisp ever so slightly.

2   tablespoons unsalted butter, plus more for brushing

2   tablespoons extra-virgin olive oil, plus more for drizzling

1   pound mixed wild mushrooms, such as stemmed and sliced shiitake, quartered cremini, and oyster mushrooms, cut into 1-inch pieces

    Kosher salt and freshly ground black pepper

1   tablespoon fresh lemon juice

¼   cup distilled white vinegar

4   large eggs

4   (½-inch-thick) slices sourdough boule

¼   cup torn fresh basil leaves

In a large nonstick skillet, melt the butter in the olive oil over medium-high heat. Add the mushrooms and a generous pinch each of salt and pepper. Toss quickly, cover, and cook, undisturbed, until the mushrooms are tender and lightly browned on the bottom, about 8 minutes. Transfer to a medium bowl, stir in the lemon juice, and season with salt and pepper. Cover with plastic wrap to keep warm.

Wipe out the skillet. Fill the skillet with water and heat over medium heat until tiny bubbles appear on the bottom. Stir in the vinegar and a generous pinch of salt. One at a time, crack the eggs into a small bowl and very carefully slide them into the water. Poach over medium heat until the whites are just firm and the yolks are runny, 3 to 5 minutes. Using a slotted spoon, transfer the eggs to a plate.

Meanwhile, toast and butter the bread and then transfer to plates. Stir the basil into the mushrooms and spoon onto the toasts. Carefully slide the poached eggs onto the toasts over the mushrooms. Drizzle with olive oil and sprinkle with salt and pepper. Serve with a knife and fork.

DO IT AHEAD   The cooked mushrooms can be refrigerated in an airtight container overnight. Reheat them gently and stir in the basil before serving.

MINI BLUEBERRY-GINGER BREAKFAST BUNS

HANDS-ON TIME
15 MIN

TOTAL TIME
50 MIN

MAKES 12 MINI
BUNS

Keep these adorable pastries on hand to serve surprise visitors, reward your kids, and treat yo'self. The recipe is easy because all you need are a few pantry staples, and brilliant because the sugars at the bottom of the muffin cups become crunchy and caramelized. I like to sprinkle a few dried blueberries on the pastry before rolling it up, but chopped dried cranberries work well, too, or feel free to skip the fruit altogether.

Buns

- 2 tablespoons cold unsalted butter, cut into 12 cubes
- All-purpose flour, for dusting
- 1 (8-ounce) sheet frozen puff pastry, thawed
- ⅓ cup blueberry preserves
- ¼ cup dried blueberries or chopped dried cranberries
- 2 tablespoons packed light brown sugar
- ¾ teaspoon ground ginger

Icing

- ½ cup confectioners' sugar
- 1 tablespoon unsalted butter, melted
- ¼ teaspoon ground ginger
- Pinch of kosher salt

Make the buns Preheat the oven to 325°F. Divide the cubed butter evenly among the cups of a 12-cup muffin pan.

On a lightly floured work surface, unfold the sheet of puff pastry and roll it out to a 12-inch-long rectangle. Using a small offset spatula, spread the blueberry preserves evenly over the puff pastry, leaving a ½-inch border. Sprinkle the dried blueberries, brown sugar, and ginger evenly on top. Loosely roll up the puff pastry to form a log. Using a sharp knife, cut off ½ inch from each end of the log and then cut the log crosswise into 12 even buns. Transfer the buns cut-side down to the prepared muffin pan.

Bake the buns for about 45 minutes, until puffed and golden. Let cool in the muffin pan for 5 minutes and then invert them onto a waxed paper–lined baking sheet to cool slightly.

Meanwhile, make the icing In a medium bowl, whisk together the confectioners' sugar, melted butter, ginger, and salt until thick and smooth. Spread the icing on the warm buns and serve.

COCONUT-LIME
MUFFINS

HANDS-ON TIME
20 MIN

TOTAL TIME
45 MIN PLUS
COOLING

MAKES 18
MUFFINS

Sometimes baked goods made with shredded coconut can taste artificial or overpowering. I've learned that unsweetened coconut flakes or chips, which are thicker and not as wet, produce a natural, more delicate flavor as well as an incredible texture. Here I pair the coconut flakes with unsweetened coconut milk to make a super-tender and moist muffin.

1¼ cups all-purpose flour

¾ teaspoon baking powder

½ teaspoon baking soda

½ teaspoon kosher salt

½ cup (1 stick) unsalted butter, at room temperature or softened in the microwave

¾ cup sugar

1 large egg

¾ cup unsweetened coconut milk

3 tablespoons packed finely grated lime zest

1 teaspoon pure vanilla extract

2 cups unsweetened coconut flakes or chips (not shredded), such as Bob's Red Mill

Preheat the oven to 350°F. Line 18 cups of two 12-cup muffin pans with paper or foil liners.

In a medium bowl, whisk together the flour, baking powder, baking soda, and salt. In a large bowl, using a handheld mixer, beat the butter with the sugar on medium-high speed until fluffy, 1 to 2 minutes. Beat in the egg until incorporated, then beat in the coconut milk, lime zest, and vanilla until smooth. Add the flour mixture and beat on low speed until the batter is just smooth, about 1 minute.

Divide the batter evenly among the prepared muffin cups and sprinkle each with 2 tablespoons of the coconut flakes. Bake for 20 to 25 minutes, until the muffins have risen and a toothpick inserted into the center of a muffin comes out clean. Transfer the muffins to a wire rack to cool before serving.

DO IT AHEAD The muffins can be stored in an airtight container at room temperature overnight.

MASA
PANCAKES
with Spiced Butter

HANDS-ON TIME
35 MIN

TOTAL TIME
35 MIN

SERVES 4

This recipe honors the cinnamon toast I loved as a kid as well as one of my favorite breakfast foods of all time, pancakes. I combine all-purpose flour with masa harina (the very finely ground corn flour used to make tortillas) to give the pancakes a robust, earthy flavor that's just so good with the warm spices in the butter.

Spiced Butter

- ½ cup (1 stick) unsalted butter, at room temperature or softened in the microwave
- 2 tablespoons sugar
- 2 teaspoons ground cinnamon
- 1 teaspoon ground ginger
- 1 teaspoon ancho chile powder or chili powder
- ¼ teaspoon kosher salt
- Pinch of ground nutmeg

Pancakes

- 1 cup all-purpose flour
- 1 cup masa harina
- 2 tablespoons sugar
- 1 teaspoon kosher salt
- 1 teaspoon baking powder
- ½ teaspoon baking soda
- 2 large eggs
- 2½ cups buttermilk
- 2 tablespoons canola or vegetable oil, plus more for greasing
- Warm maple syrup, for serving

Make the spiced butter In a small bowl, using a fork, blend together the butter, sugar, cinnamon, ginger, chile powder, salt, and nutmeg.

Make the pancakes Preheat the oven to 200°F.

In a large bowl, whisk together the flour, masa, sugar, salt, baking powder, and baking soda. In another bowl, whisk together the eggs, buttermilk, and canola oil. Stir the egg mixture into the flour mixture just until combined.

Heat a large nonstick or cast-iron skillet over medium heat. Brush the skillet with canola oil. Scoop three ⅓-cup mounds of the batter into the skillet, spreading them slightly. Cook until bubbles appear on the surface, about 3 minutes. Flip the pancakes and cook until they are golden brown on the bottom, about 2 minutes longer. Transfer to a baking sheet and put it in the oven to keep warm. Repeat with the remaining batter.

Serve the pancakes with the spiced butter and warm maple syrup.

BREAKFAST PIZZA

(aka Dad's Breakfast Pizza)

HANDS-ON TIME
30 MIN

TOTAL TIME
45 MIN

SERVES 4 TO 6

My dad pretty much cooked two things on a regular basis: BBQ chicken and breakfast pizza. Actually, it wasn't so much a pizza as it was a frittata, but that's what he always called it, and I'm sticking with it. Sautéed potatoes, onions, and eggs form the "crust," with shredded mozzarella and sliced pepperoni as the toppings. As with real pizza, it's delicious hot or not, but at room temperature it's certainly easier to eat with your hands.

¼ cup extra-virgin olive oil

1 pound red potatoes, cut into ½-inch pieces

1 red onion, finely chopped

⅓ cup chopped pepperoni slices, plus 16 whole slices (about 7 ounces total)

2 garlic cloves, minced

Kosher salt and freshly ground black pepper

8 large eggs

1½ cups shredded mozzarella (6 ounces)

Dried oregano, for sprinkling

Red pepper flakes, for sprinkling

Preheat the oven to 450°F.

In a large nonstick or cast-iron skillet, heat the olive oil over medium-high heat until shimmering. Add the potatoes, onion, chopped pepperoni, garlic, and a generous pinch each of salt and pepper. Cook, stirring occasionally, until the vegetables are softened and just lightly brown, about 15 minutes.

Meanwhile, in a large bowl, beat the eggs with a generous pinch each of salt and black pepper.

Add the eggs to the skillet and cook, stirring and shaking the pan, until the eggs just start to set, about 3 minutes. Remove from the heat and, using a rubber spatula, smooth the top. Scatter the cheese evenly over the top, then top with the pepperoni slices. Transfer to the oven and bake for 7 minutes, until the cheese has melted and the eggs are cooked through. Let stand for 5 minutes.

Sprinkle with dried oregano and red pepper flakes, then cut into wedges and serve.

CROQUE MADAME
HOT DISH

HANDS-ON TIME
35 MIN

TOTAL TIME
1 HR 10 MIN

SERVES 6

Croque monsieur is a classic French sandwich filled with ham and bathed in a warm, cheesy béchamel sauce. Add a fried egg and you've got croque madame. I've made this sandwich endlessly, but never for a group because you can only prepare them one at a time. Then I created this casserole—aka "hot dish," the Midwestern term—of white toast layered with béchamel, ham, and shredded Gruyère and topped with a few runny eggs.

4   tablespoons (½ stick) unsalted butter, plus more for greasing

10   slices white country bread, halved

¼   cup all-purpose flour

3   cups whole milk

2   tablespoons Dijon mustard

   Kosher salt and freshly ground black pepper

½   pound thinly sliced ham, such as Virginia or Black Forest, coarsely chopped

8   ounces Gruyère cheese, shredded (2 cups)

6   large eggs

Preheat the oven to 375°F. Generously grease a 9 by 13-inch glass or ceramic baking dish with butter.

Spread the bread on a large baking sheet and bake for about 10 minutes, until dry and very lightly toasted.

Meanwhile, in a medium saucepan, melt the butter over medium-high heat. Add the flour and cook, whisking continuously, until a paste forms and it starts to bubble, about 2 minutes. Gradually whisk in the milk until smooth. Bring the sauce to a boil and then simmer over medium-low heat until thickened and no floury taste remains, about 7 minutes. Whisk in the mustard and season the sauce with salt and pepper.

Spread ½ cup of the sauce in the prepared baking dish. Arrange half the toast in the baking dish and spread half the remaining sauce on top. Scatter half the ham and cheese on the coated bread. Repeat the layering one more time with the remaining bread, sauce, ham, and cheese.

Bake the hot dish for 15 minutes, until hot and the cheese has melted. One at a time, crack the eggs onto the hot dish so that the whites spread a little and the yolks sit in little divots. Bake the hot dish for 12 to 15 minutes more, just until the egg whites are just set but the yolks are still runny. Serve hot.

DO IT AHEAD   You can make the creamy sauce the day before and store it in an airtight container in the refrigerator. Reheat it gently in the microwave before assembling the casserole.

BLUEBERRY-VANILLA
BREKFAST CEREAL

with Yogurt & Blueberry Preserves

HANDS-ON TIME
15 MIN

TOTAL TIME
55 MIN PLUS
COOLING

MAKES 8 CUPS
(2¼ POUNDS)

I eat a lot of yogurt when I'm working, but without something crunchy on top I'm just not satisfied. That's where this breakfast cereal comes in. I always have some in my pantry and even in my freezer for when the need arises. Sometimes I'll skip the yogurt and just pour some in a big bowl with milk, which is why I call it cereal and not granola, but you can call it whatever you want.

4	cups old-fashioned rolled oats (1 pound)
¾	cup packed light brown sugar
¾	cup all-purpose flour
1	teaspoon kosher salt
¾	cup (1½ sticks) unsalted butter
½	cup pure maple syrup
¼	cup honey
1	vanilla bean, split and seeds scraped out, or 1 teaspoon pure vanilla extract
1	cup dried blueberries (6 ounces)
	Plain Greek yogurt and blueberry jam, for serving

Preheat the oven to 300°F. Line a large rimmed baking sheet with parchment paper.

In a large bowl, toss the oats, brown sugar, flour, and salt until well mixed.

In a small saucepan, melt the butter over low heat. Whisk in the maple syrup, honey, and vanilla. Scrape the butter mixture into the bowl with the oat mixture and, using a rubber spatula, mix until the oats are evenly coated. Spread the oats in an even layer on the prepared baking sheet.

Bake the cereal for about 20 minutes, stirring two or three times, until golden and almost dry. Stir in the blueberries and bake for 5 minutes more. Let the cereal cool completely, stirring occasionally to break up the clumps, before serving.

Spoon some yogurt into bowls. Top with some cereal and jam and serve.

DO IT AHEAD The cereal can be stored in an airtight container at room temperature for up to 2 weeks.

QUICK-PICKLED GRAPE TOMATOES
ON RICOTTA TOAST

HANDS-ON TIME
15 MIN

TOTAL TIME
2 HRS 15 MIN

SERVES 4

When I studied at The French Culinary Institute in New York City, I cooked at the FCI's restaurant, L'Ecole, as part of the curriculum. I worked the fish station for a while, and it was one of the most challenging spots because there were so many ways to mess up! But the pickled grape tomatoes we served with the sea bass were idiot-proof, and great for snacking. I loved how they burst in my mouth with all sorts of tangy-sweet flavors. We always peeled the grape tomatoes back then, but nowadays I usually just poke them all over with a toothpick and pop them into a hot brine. They're great right out of the fridge and in salads, but in my opinion, the best way to serve them is on ricotta toast, drizzled with olive oil.

1 pint grape tomatoes

1 cup unseasoned rice vinegar

2 tablespoons sugar

2 large garlic cloves, crushed

2 fresh thyme sprigs

½ jalapeño

   Kosher salt

1½ cups whole-milk ricotta cheese

4 thick slices sourdough boule or other rustic bread, lightly toasted or grilled

   Extra-virgin olive oil, for drizzling

   Freshly ground black pepper

Using a toothpick, poke a few holes all over each tomato. In a medium saucepan, combine the vinegar, sugar, garlic, thyme, jalapeño, ½ cup water, and 1 tablespoon salt and bring to a boil over high heat. Add the tomatoes and return to a boil, then remove from the heat and let cool completely, about 1 hour. Transfer to a jar or container with a tight-fitting lid and refrigerate until well chilled, about 1 hour.

Spread the ricotta evenly on the toasts. Using a slotted spoon, top the toasts with the tomatoes and a little bit of their pickling liquid. Drizzle with olive oil and season with pepper.

DO IT AHEAD The pickled tomatoes can be refrigerated in their pickling liquid for up to 2 weeks.

WHITE CHEDDAR FAUXFFLÉ

HANDS-ON TIME
35 MIN

TOTAL TIME
1 HR 45 MIN

SERVES 4

We didn't have much money when I was growing up, so we ate a lot of eggs. My grandma Barbara would do incredible things with them. Her soufflé was a cheater's version that she made without separating the whites and yolks. She just beat the heck out of those eggs, then baked them in a dish coated with butter and bread crumbs. If we were lucky enough to have American or Monterey Jack cheese on hand, she'd add that, too. It was basically an egg casserole that felt special because it reminded me of what I'd see on TV prepared by the Two Fat Ladies or Jacques Pépin. Years later, I've become friends with Jacques's daughter, Claudine, who told me her father would often make his soufflé without separating the eggs, too. So, as it turns out, Grandma shared her technique with an OG of French cuisine.

6 tablespoons (¾ stick) unsalted butter, plus more for greasing

¼ cup plain dry bread crumbs

⅓ cup all-purpose flour

2 cups whole milk

4 ounces sharp white cheddar, shredded (1 cup)

2 tablespoons minced fresh chives

2 tablespoons minced fresh parsley

2 tablespoons minced fresh dill

Kosher salt and freshly ground black pepper

6 large eggs

Preheat the oven to 375°F. Grease a 1½-quart soufflé or deep baking dish with butter (I use a stoneware baking dish that's about 9 by 7 inches and 2 inches deep).

Add the bread crumbs and turn the baking dish to coat the bottom and sides; shake out the excess. Set the dish on a rimmed baking sheet.

In a medium saucepan, melt the butter over medium heat. Add the flour and cook, whisking, until a bubbling paste forms, about 2 minutes. Whisking continuously, very gradually drizzle in the milk until smooth. Bring the sauce to a simmer, then cook over medium-low heat, whisking frequently, until thickened and no floury taste remains, about 7 minutes. Scrape into a large bowl and let cool, about 10 minutes. Stir in the cheddar, chives, parsley, and dill. Season generously with salt and pepper.

In another large bowl, using a whisk, beat the eggs until very frothy. Whisk one-third of the beaten eggs into the sauce mixture to lighten it, then fold in the remaining beaten eggs until incorporated.

Scrape the fauxfflé base into the prepared baking dish. Bake for about 1 hour, until risen and browned on top. Serve the fauxfflé right away.

VARIATION For a fun riff on cacio e pepe, substitute grated Parmesan for half the shredded cheddar. Instead of herbs, stir 1½ tablespoons coarsely ground black pepper into the base and then sprinkle the top with more pepper before baking.

FRENCH TOAST
CASSEROLE
with Caramelized Peaches

HANDS-ON TIME
30 MIN

TOTAL TIME
1 HR
15 MIN PLUS
OVERNIGHT
SOAKING

SERVES 6 TO 8

French toast is just not my thing. I simply don't see the appeal of standing over the stove cooking one sopping wet piece of bread at a time while everybody sits around waiting. I don't even order French toast at restaurants. However, breakfast casseroles are *totally* my thing. They're easy, they're make-ahead, and they bring a little family-style love and togetherness to the table. Thus, my French toast casserole, which involves combining all the usual suspects (bread, milk, eggs, vanilla, sugar) and letting everything soak overnight before baking. I call for sourdough here—not sure if you've noticed that I use sourdough *all the time*—although thick-cut challah works, too. If you're in a hurry, you can skip the caramelized peaches and just spread on some fruit jam.

2 tablespoons unsalted butter, plus more for greasing

1 (1¼-pound) sourdough boule or challah, cut into 1-inch-thick slices

6 large eggs

2 cups whole milk

½ cup heavy cream

½ cup granulated sugar

1 vanilla bean, split and seeds scraped out, or 1 teaspoon pure vanilla extract

1 teaspoon finely grated lemon zest

Kosher salt

3 firm but ripe peaches, cut into ½-inch wedges (see Tip)

¼ cup packed light brown sugar

Warm maple syrup, for serving

Confectioners' sugar, for dusting

Butter a 9 by 13-inch oval baking dish and then arrange the bread in slightly overlapping layers in it.

In a large bowl, beat the eggs, milk, cream, granulated sugar, vanilla bean seeds or extract, lemon zest, and ½ teaspoon salt. Pour the egg mixture over the bread, gently pressing the bread to submerge it. Cover with plastic wrap and refrigerate until the egg mixture has been absorbed by the bread, at least 1 hour but preferably overnight.

Preheat the oven to 350°F.

Uncover the baking dish and bake for 45 to 55 minutes, until the center is set but slightly jiggly. Let stand for 10 minutes.

RECIPE CONTINUES

Meanwhile, in a large skillet, melt the butter over medium-high heat. Add the peaches, brown sugar, and a pinch of salt. Cook, stirring occasionally, until the peaches are tender and browned in spots, 5 to 7 minutes.

Serve the French toast with the caramelized peaches and warm maple syrup, dusted with confectioners' sugar.

TIP Cutting a peach into wedges—especially when the fruit is still a bit firm—can feel cumbersome. But it doesn't need to be. Do what I do: Cut the peach into wedges while it's still on the pit! Using a paring knife, cut one ½-inch wedge lengthwise into a peach and then wiggle the knife while twisting the knife up to release the wedge. Continue the process all the way around the pit until you cut off your last wedge.

SOUPS & STEWS

EVERYBODY ALWAYS DESCRIBES SOUPS AND STEWS in the same boring way: *soulful*, *comforting*, *hearty*, and so forth until I want to put my head down on the kitchen counter and take a little nap. Wake up, people! Why stick with the same old, same old? I hope you find the recipes in this chapter as fun as I do. I use a bunch of shortcuts to create awesome new bowls of goodness, like my smoky marinara soup, which gets a little—actually, a ton—of help from jarred tomato sauce (page 89) or my super-tasty Asian stew that uses store-bought Chinese dumplings (page 100). Sometimes I rely on time-saving methods. For my updated beef bourguignon (page 102), for instance, I harness the power of a kitchen tool you probably don't turn to as often as you should: the broiler.

Smoky
MARINARA SOUP
with Garlic Bread Croutons
89

LIME SOUP
with Chicken & Hearty Greens
90

Kimchi &
SILKEN TOFU STEW
91

YELLOW
GAZPACHO
with Smoked Almond & Parsley Gremolata
92

Red Curry
PEANUT SOUP
with Chicken
94

BACON-&-EGG
RAMEN
in Buttery Broth
97

Easiest
FISH STEW
with Pickled-Pepper Rouille
98

WHITE CHICKEN
CHILI
with Poblanos & Hominy
99

Shumai
STEW
with Shiitake & Mustard Greens
100

NEW-SCHOOL
BEEF BOURGUIGNON
102

Farro & Black Bean
CHILI
with Swiss Chard & Jack Cheese
105

Double
BEET SOUP
106

All-Day
CASSOULET
107

SLOW-COOKED LAMB & SWEET POTATO
CURRY
108

SMOKY MARINARA SOUP

with Garlic Bread Croutons

HANDS-ON TIME
15 MIN

TOTAL TIME
30 MIN

SERVES 4

Go ahead and call me a cheater, but I have no problem using jarred marinara sauce as the key ingredient in this fast tomato soup. I love a supermarket brand called Rao's, from the hyper-exclusive New York City restaurant I dream of visiting one day when I become a sports star or a big-deal politico (no one else can get in). Rao's marinara is packed with aromatics and seasonings, with no preservatives or sugar, and it is literally incredible. Combine it with chicken broth, smoked sweet paprika, and a teeny bit of butter, if you'd like, and you will feel like you've gotten away with a minor crime—it's that easy and that good.

¼ cup plus 2 tablespoons extra-virgin olive oil

1 large onion, finely chopped

4 garlic cloves, minced

1 (24-ounce) jar good-quality marinara sauce, such as Rao's

3 cups low-sodium chicken broth

1 fresh basil sprig, plus torn leaves for topping

1 tablespoon smoked sweet paprika

2 tablespoons unsalted butter (optional)

Kosher salt and freshly ground black pepper

1 (8-ounce) loaf rustic bread, such as ciabatta, baguette, or sourdough, cut into 1-inch cubes

½ teaspoon garlic powder with parsley

Grated Parmesan cheese, for topping

Preheat the oven to 425°F.

In a large saucepan, heat 2 tablespoons of the olive oil over medium heat. Add the onion and garlic and cook, stirring occasionally, until softened, about 8 minutes. Stir in the marinara sauce, broth, basil sprig, and paprika. Simmer until bubbling and thickened slightly, about 8 minutes. Stir in the butter (if using) until melted, then season the soup with salt and pepper. Keep warm over very low heat.

Meanwhile, on a large rimmed baking sheet, toss the bread cubes with the remaining ¼ cup olive oil, the garlic powder, and a generous pinch each of salt and pepper. Bake for about 10 minutes, until crispy on the edges but still chewy in the middle.

Spoon the soup into bowls. Top with the croutons, torn basil, and grated Parmesan. Serve right away.

DO IT AHEAD The soup can be refrigerated in an airtight container for up to 3 days. The croutons can be stored in an airtight container at room temperature overnight. Reheat the soup in a saucepan over medium heat, stirring occasionally until hot, before serving.

LIME SOUP

with Chicken & Hearty Greens

HANDS-ON TIME
25 MIN

TOTAL TIME
30 MIN

SERVES 4

One year, my friend Steve invited a bunch of us to his epic birthday party in Mexico. Sure, I loved the margaritas, but what really blew me away was *the soup*. The restaurant at our hotel served an unbelievable *sopa de lima*—a simple, tangy, crazy-flavorful, lime-spiked broth with little pieces of shredded chicken. I make my version quite a bit because it's so fast, delicious, and healthy. I've added some stuff along the way, like jalapeño and mustard greens (kale or even Swiss chard works well, too).

2 tablespoons extra-virgin olive oil

1 white onion, finely chopped

2 medium tomatoes, finely diced

6 garlic cloves, thinly sliced

1 jalapeño, halved lengthwise, seeded, and thinly sliced

Kosher salt and freshly ground black pepper

1 quart low-sodium chicken broth

4 cups shredded cooked chicken (from 1 small rotisserie chicken)

4 cups torn mustard greens or kale (4 ounces)

¼ cup plus 2 tablespoons fresh lime juice

Chopped fresh cilantro, for topping

Diced Hass avocado, for topping

In a large saucepan, heat the olive oil over medium heat. Add the onion, tomatoes, garlic, jalapeño, and a generous pinch each of salt and pepper. Cook, stirring occasionally, until the onion is just softened and the tomatoes start to break down, about 8 minutes. Add the broth and bring to a boil over high heat, then simmer over medium heat for 5 minutes. Stir in the chicken, greens, and lime juice, then season the soup with salt and pepper. Ladle into bowls and top with chopped cilantro and avocado. Serve hot.

KIMCHI & SILKEN TOFU STEW

HANDS-ON TIME
30 MIN

TOTAL TIME
45 MIN

SERVES 4

Kimchi, the spicy, garlicky, pungent Korean condiment, deserves its own spot in your fridge, if it isn't there already. Just a little stirred into a soup or stew provides a humongous flavor boost. The recipe here is proof. Typically, Koreans prepare this dish with pork, but to make it super easy and fast I just stir in some cubed tofu and call it a day (you could also add some shredded rotisserie chicken). I eat this stew whenever I feel like my body needs a wake-up call; it's especially effective as a hangover cure.

1   (15-ounce) jar kimchi

2   tablespoons canola oil

1   yellow onion, finely chopped

4   garlic cloves, minced

2   tablespoons peeled and minced fresh ginger

    Kosher salt

2   tablespoons gochujang (Korean red pepper paste) or sriracha

1   tablespoon low-sodium soy sauce

1   quart low-sodium chicken broth

1   (14-ounce) package silken tofu, drained and cut into 1-inch pieces

6   scallions, thinly sliced, plus more for sprinkling

2   tablespoons unsalted butter (optional)

Drain the kimchi in a colander set over a bowl. Squeeze out and reserve as much of the juice as possible, then finely chop the kimchi.

In a large saucepan, heat the canola oil over medium-high heat. Add the onion, garlic, ginger, and a generous pinch of salt and cook, stirring occasionally, until the onion is softened and lightly browned, about 8 minutes. Add the chopped kimchi, gochujang, and soy sauce and cook, stirring, until hot, about 2 minutes. Add the broth and the reserved kimchi juice and bring just to a boil. Simmer over medium-low heat, stirring occasionally, until the kimchi is softened slightly, about 15 minutes. Stir in the tofu, scallions, and butter (if using), then simmer until the tofu is hot, about 5 minutes longer. Season the stew lightly with salt.

Ladle the stew into bowls, sprinkle with sliced scallions, and serve.

DO IT AHEAD   The stew can be refrigerated in an airtight container for up to 3 days. Reheat in a saucepan over medium heat, stirring occasionally, until hot.

YELLOW GAZPACHO

with Smoked Almond & Parsley Gremolata

HANDS-ON TIME
15 MIN

TOTAL TIME
1 HR 15 MIN

SERVES 4 AS
A STARTER

Does the thought of using yellow tomatoes here instead of the usual red ones make you gasp? Take my advice: Don't be afraid to be different! I'm not (or at least I try not to be). Yellow tomatoes tend to be slightly sweeter and less acidic. Plus, they puree into a brilliant color that transforms a classic soup into something new and thrilling. Here, a small amount of turmeric not only bumps up the beautiful golden color but also makes the recipe even healthier.

3	(10-ounce) containers yellow or gold grape tomatoes
2	garlic cloves, crushed
¼	teaspoon turmeric powder
¼	teaspoon freshly ground white pepper
¼	cup extra-virgin olive oil, plus more for drizzling
	Kosher salt
½	cup smoked almonds
½	cup lightly packed fresh parsley leaves
¾	teaspoon finely grated lemon zest

In a blender or food processor, combine the tomatoes, 2 tablespoons water, 1 garlic clove, the turmeric, and the white pepper and puree until the gazpacho is very smooth (you want to break down the skins as much as possible to give you a gorgeous color), 1 to 2 minutes. With the machine on, drizzle in the olive oil until emulsified. Season the soup generously with salt. Transfer to an airtight container and refrigerate for 1 hour.

In a food processor (a little one works great here), combine the almonds, parsley, lemon zest, the remaining garlic clove, and a generous pinch of salt. Pulse until the almonds and parsley are finely chopped. Transfer to a small bowl.

Ladle the gazpacho into bowls. Sprinkle some of the gremolata on top and drizzle with a little olive oil. Serve right away, passing more gremolata at the table.

DO IT AHEAD The gazpacho can be refrigerated in an airtight container for up to 3 days.

RED CURRY PEANUT SOUP

with Chicken

TOTAL TIME
45 MIN

SERVES 6 TO 8

I know it sounds nuts, but peanut butter goes as well with savory ingredients as sweet ones—if you've ever had chicken satay with peanut sauce at a Thai restaurant, you get my point. Still not convinced? Then try this soup, a West African classic mashed up with a few Thai flavors. You can buy pretty much all the ingredients at the supermarket; even the red curry paste is available at more and more grocers, as well as at Asian markets and online retailers like Amazon.

2 tablespoons canola or vegetable oil

1 pound boneless, skinless chicken thighs, cut into ¾-inch pieces

Kosher salt and freshly ground black pepper

1 large onion, finely chopped

2 jalapeños, seeded and minced

2 tablespoons peeled and minced fresh ginger

2 garlic cloves, minced

1½ tablespoons Thai red curry paste

2 plum tomatoes, finely chopped

1 cup smooth peanut butter

1 tablespoon sugar

1 quart low-sodium chicken broth

1 tablespoon soy sauce

3 tablespoons fresh lime juice

1½ teaspoons sriracha, plus more for serving

Chopped roasted peanuts, for sprinkling

Fresh cilantro, for sprinkling

Lime wedges, for serving

In a large saucepan, heat the canola oil over medium heat. Season the chicken with salt and pepper and add it to the saucepan. Cook, stirring, until lightly browned but not cooked through, about 5 minutes. Using a slotted spoon, transfer the chicken to a plate.

Add the onion, jalapeños, ginger, and garlic to the saucepan and cook over medium heat, stirring occasionally, until the vegetables are softened and just starting to brown, about 8 minutes. Stir in the red curry paste and cook until the vegetables are coated, about 1 minute. Stir in the tomatoes, peanut butter, and sugar and cook over medium-low heat, stirring, until the peanut butter has melted. Whisk in the broth and soy sauce and bring to a boil.

Return the chicken to the saucepan and simmer over medium-low heat until the chicken is cooked through and the soup is hot, about 12 minutes. Stir in the lime juice and sriracha and season with salt and pepper.

Ladle the soup into bowls and sprinkle with chopped roasted peanuts and cilantro. Serve with lime wedges and sriracha.

DO IT AHEAD   The peanut soup can be refrigerated in an airtight container overnight. Reheat in a saucepan over medium heat, stirring occasionally, until hot; add a bit of water if too thick.

BACON-&-EGG
RAMEN

in Buttery Broth

HANDS-ON TIME
20 MIN

TOTAL TIME
40 MIN

SERVES 4

Whenever I see instant ramen at the store, I think about the meals I ate when I first moved to New York . . . and Grandma Barbara. When I was growing up, she'd break the noodles into a bowl of water, crack an egg on top, and microwave the whole thing. Showered with thinly sliced scallions (or green onions, as she'd call them), it was one of the most satisfying meals of my childhood.

Another time Grandma pan-fried finely crushed ramen noodles in bacon fat until richly browned and then simmered them in chicken broth until the mixture resembled thick porridge. It might not sound beautiful, but it sure was tasty, especially with some sliced radishes and chopped tomatoes on top.

My bacon-and-egg ramen was inspired by my grandma's brilliance. I simmer bacon in water to make a fast, full-flavored ramen broth and then finish the whole thing with poached eggs, thinly sliced mushrooms, and scallions.

1 quart low-sodium chicken broth

1 (4-ounce) piece slab bacon

3 (3-ounce) packages chicken-flavored ramen with their seasoning packets

2 tablespoons unsalted butter

1 tablespoon sambal oelek or other Asian chile paste, plus more for serving

4 large eggs

Thinly sliced button mushrooms, for serving

Thinly sliced scallions, for serving

In a large saucepan, combine the broth, bacon, ramen seasoning packets, and 4 cups water and bring to a boil over high heat. Cover and simmer over medium-low heat until the bacon is tender, about 20 minutes. Transfer the bacon to a work surface and cut it into ¼-inch-thick slices.

Break the ramen noodles in half and add them to the saucepan along with the butter and sambal oelek. Simmer over medium heat, stirring occasionally, until the noodles just start to soften, about 1 minute. One at a time, crack the eggs into a small bowl and very carefully slide them on top of the noodles. Let them poach, undisturbed, until the whites are just firm but the yolks are runny, about 4 minutes.

Transfer the noodles, eggs, and bacon to four bowls and ladle the broth on top. Top the ramen with thinly sliced mushrooms and scallions. Serve hot, passing additional sambal oelek at the table.

EASIEST
FISH STEW

with Pickled-Pepper Rouille

HANDS-ON TIME
35 MIN

TOTAL TIME
45 MIN

SERVES 4

The secret to this fast stew is bottled clam juice. I mean it: There are three full bottles in here! It's so good with the shrimp, cod, fennel, sausage, and other big-flavored ingredients, not to mention the pickled-pepper rouille that is (for me) the best part of the dish. I also love how flexible the recipe is. When I make it for friends, I sometimes prepare it halfway, stopping before I add the fish. Then I let it hang out on the stove until we're ready to eat, at which point I heat it up again, slide in the fish to cook for a few minutes, then serve.

¼ cup extra-virgin olive oil

1 (5-ounce) sweet Italian sausage, preferably with fennel, removed from casing

1 medium onion, finely chopped

1 small fennel bulb, halved, cored, and finely chopped, fronds reserved

6 garlic cloves, thinly sliced

Kosher salt

½ cup dry white wine

1 (15-ounce) can crushed tomatoes

3 (8-ounce) bottles clam juice

Freshly ground black pepper

1 pound skinless cod fillet, cut into 1½-inch pieces

12 large shrimp, peeled and deveined

Toasted baguette slices, for serving

Pickled Pepper Rouille (page 278), for serving

In a large saucepan, heat the olive oil over medium heat. Add the sausage and cook, breaking up the meat with a wooden spoon, until nearly cooked through, 5 to 7 minutes. Add the onion, fennel, garlic, and a generous pinch of salt and cook, stirring occasionally, until the vegetables are softened, about 8 minutes. Add the wine and simmer until evaporated, about 3 minutes. Add the tomatoes and cook, stirring occasionally, until thickened slightly, 3 to 5 minutes.

Stir in the clam juice and bring to a boil over high heat. Season the broth with salt and black pepper. Nestle the cod and shrimp in the broth, then cover the saucepan and simmer over medium heat until the seafood is just cooked through, about 5 minutes.

Ladle the fish stew into shallow bowls and sprinkle fennel fronds on top. Serve with toasted baguette slices and Pickled Pepper Rouille.

WHITE CHICKEN CHILI

with Poblanos & Hominy

TOTAL TIME
30 MIN

SERVES 6

Hominy has been one of my favorites since third grade, when for some reason our teacher made the entire class try it with maple syrup (yum!) or salt and pepper. Here the puffy, chewy corn kernels replace the beans in a fast chili, adding an amazing tortilla-like flavor. The recipe also takes advantage of boneless, skinless chicken breast, not usually my go-to ingredient, but great here because it cooks quickly and absorbs all the other flavors so well.

2 tablespoons extra-virgin olive oil

1 large onion, finely chopped

2 poblano peppers, seeded and diced

2 jalapeños, seeded and minced

2 garlic cloves, minced

Kosher salt and freshly ground black pepper

1½ teaspoons ground cumin

½ teaspoon ground coriander

1½ pounds boneless, skinless chicken breasts, cut into ½-inch pieces

2½ cups low-sodium chicken broth

2 (15-ounce) cans white hominy, drained and rinsed

¼ cup sour cream, plus more for topping

Chopped fresh cilantro, for topping

Thinly sliced radishes, for topping

In a large saucepan, heat the olive oil over medium heat until shimmering. Add the onion, poblanos, jalapeños, garlic, and a generous pinch each of salt and black pepper. Cook, stirring occasionally, until the vegetables are softened but not browned, about 8 minutes. Stir in the cumin and coriander and cook until fragrant, about 2 minutes.

Add the chicken and cook, stirring, until it just starts to turn white, 3 to 5 minutes. Add the broth and hominy and bring to a boil. Simmer over medium-low heat until the chicken is just cooked through, about 8 minutes. Stir in the sour cream and season with salt and black pepper.

Ladle the chili into bowls and top with chopped cilantro, thinly sliced radishes, and a dollop of sour cream.

DO IT AHEAD The chili can be refrigerated in an airtight container for up to 2 days. Reheat in a saucepan over medium-low heat, stirring occasionally, until just hot. You don't want to dry out that lean chicken!

SHUMAI STEW

with Shiitake & Mustard Greens

HANDS-ON TIME
25 MIN

TOTAL TIME
45 MIN

SERVES 4

I once picked up a package of frozen cooked shumai from the corner convenience store because I had, ahem, a midnight craving. They were a bit on the dry side so I only ate half. But I didn't want to waste them, so I came up with this super aromatic stew. I've tried the recipe with frozen potstickers, too, and the results are just as good. If you prefer to make your own shumai, you should use my recipe (page 56) because they are a stupendous compliment to the 'shroomy broth and spicy greens.

2 tablespoons canola or vegetable oil

3 large shallots, thinly sliced lengthwise

1 (3-inch) piece fresh ginger, peeled and cut into thin matchsticks (½ cup)

6 garlic cloves, thinly sliced

Kosher salt and freshly ground white pepper

1 quart low-sodium chicken broth

1 (1-ounce) package dried shiitake mushrooms

20 frozen cooked pork shumai or gyoza (about 12 ounces)

1 (8-ounce) bunch mustard greens, stemmed, leaves chopped

1 tablespoon low-sodium soy sauce

1 tablespoon distilled white vinegar

In a large saucepan, heat the canola oil over medium heat. Add the shallots, ginger, garlic, and a generous pinch each of salt and white pepper and cook, stirring occasionally, until the vegetables are softened, about 5 minutes. Add the broth and 2 cups water and bring to a boil over high heat. Add the dried mushrooms and simmer over medium-low heat until the mushrooms are softened, 10 to 15 minutes.

Using tongs, transfer the mushrooms to a work surface. Let cool slightly, then cut off the stems and slice the caps. Return the mushrooms to the broth.

Add the shumai and simmer over medium heat until the shumai are heated through, about 5 minutes. Add the mustard greens in large handfuls and simmer until just wilted, 3 to 5 minutes. Stir in the soy sauce and vinegar. Ladle into bowls and serve.

NEW-SCHOOL BEEF BOURGUIGNON

HANDS-ON TIME
40 MIN

TOTAL TIME
3 HRS 20 MIN

SERVES 6

An old-school beef bourguignon is an incredible dish, no doubt. But it takes lots of time and effort and boy, will it mess up your stovetop. Here's what I do instead: Rather than browning the meat in batches in a skillet, splattering oil everywhere, I broil it all at once on a single large baking sheet. I use this method whenever I need to brown meat, even when I'm making something in the slow cooker, and it never fails.

4   pounds beef chuck, cut into 1-inch cubes

4   tablespoons extra-virgin olive oil

    Kosher salt and freshly ground black pepper

6   thick-cut bacon slices (6 ounces), chopped

1   large onion, finely chopped

6   garlic cloves, crushed

⅓   cup all-purpose flour

1   (750-ml) bottle dry red wine, such as Pinot Noir

1   (15-ounce) can low-sodium beef broth

2   tablespoons Worcestershire sauce

2   tablespoons tomato paste

1   pound medium carrots, cut on an angle into 2-inch pieces

1   pound baby cremini mushrooms, halved if large

½   pound small shallots, halved lengthwise

    Snipped fresh dill or parsley, for sprinkling

    Crusty bread, for serving

Preheat the broiler. Position a rack 6 to 8 inches from the heat.

On a large rimmed baking sheet, toss the beef with 2 tablespoons of the olive oil and season with salt and pepper. Broil until well browned on top, 5 to 7 minutes.

In a large pot or enameled cast-iron casserole, heat the remaining 2 tablespoons olive oil over medium-high heat. Add the bacon and cook, stirring occasionally, until browned but not crisp, about 5 minutes. Add the onion and garlic and cook, stirring occasionally, until the onion is softened, about 5 minutes. Stir in the beef and season with salt and pepper. Sprinkle the flour on top and cook, stirring, until the beef and vegetables are evenly coated, about 2 minutes.

Add the wine, broth, Worcestershire sauce, and tomato paste and bring to a boil over high heat. Reduce the heat to low, cover, and braise until the beef is tender, about 1 hour 30 minutes.

Stir the carrots, mushrooms, and shallots into the stew. Cover and braise until the beef is very tender and the vegetables are softened, about 1 hour more; uncover the pot for the last 30 minutes. Season the stew with salt and pepper.

Spoon the stew into bowls, sprinkle with dill or parsley, and serve with crusty bread.

DO IT AHEAD   The stew can be refrigerated in an airtight container for up to 3 days. Reheat in a saucepan over medium heat, stirring occasionally, until hot.

FARRO & BLACK BEAN CHILI

with Swiss Chard & Jack Cheese

HANDS-ON TIME
35 MIN

TOTAL TIME
55 MIN

SERVES 4

I am not about to argue about what makes "chili" a "chili" and not just a stew. Some people say it's gotta have meat and meat alone, while others are okay with beans. Everyone more or less agrees that a chili has to have chile peppers. So there ya go, I'm pointing to the chipotles here and calling it: This recipe is a chili. Now that we've gotten that debate out of the way, I'll bring up another point: Who woulda thought putting farro in chili could be a thing? Well, ladies and gents, *I* thought of it, and I couldn't be happier with the result. The farro adds a pleasant chew and the black beans offer a hit of lean protein.

2   tablespoons extra-virgin olive oil

4   thick-cut bacon slices, chopped

1   red onion, finely chopped

1   medium carrot, finely chopped

1   medium celery rib, finely chopped

    Kosher salt

1   cup pearled farro (aka quick-cooking farro)

1   (15-ounce) can diced tomatoes

2   canned chipotles in adobo, seeded and minced, plus 2 tablespoons adobo sauce from the can

1   quart low-sodium chicken broth

½   pound Swiss chard, thick stems trimmed, leaves and thin stems chopped

1   (15-ounce) can black beans, drained and rinsed

    Shredded Monterey Jack cheese, for sprinkling

In a large saucepan, heat the olive oil over medium heat. Add the bacon and cook, stirring occasionally, until rendered but not crisp, about 5 minutes. Add the onion, carrot, celery, and a generous pinch of salt. Cook, stirring occasionally, until the vegetables are softened, about 7 minutes. Add the farro, tomatoes, chipotles, and adobo sauce. Cook, stirring, until bubbling, about 2 minutes. Stir in the broth and bring to a boil over high heat, then cover partially and simmer over medium heat, stirring occasionally, until the farro is tender, about 20 minutes.

Stir the chard and beans into the saucepan and simmer until the chard is tender and the beans are heated through, about 5 minutes. Season the chili with salt and pepper.

Ladle the chili into bowls and serve hot, sprinkled with shredded Monterey Jack.

DO IT AHEAD   The chili can be refrigerated in an airtight container overnight. Reheat in a saucepan over medium heat, stirring occasionally, until hot; add a bit of water if too thick.

DOUBLE
BEET SOUP

HANDS-ON TIME
20 MIN

TOTAL TIME
1 HR

SERVES 4 TO 6

This recipe is based on borscht (aka *barszcz*), the beet soup found throughout eastern Europe. I'm not sure if I can call it traditional, though, because even after doing a bit of research and sifting through a lot of recipes, I haven't been able to find a single, definitive classic: The soup seems to be prepared in so many different ways in so many different places. Whatever the backstory, I really dig my version. Shredded beets lend the soup a marvelous texture; pickled beets, a sweet-sour kick. Of course beets are an acquired taste. If you like them, you'll love this recipe.

2 tablespoons extra-virgin olive oil

¾ pound fresh beets, peeled and shredded (see Note)

Kosher salt

1 quart buttermilk

½ cup sour cream

1 (16-ounce) jar pickled beets, drained and finely diced (see Tip)

2 Persian cucumbers, peeled and finely diced

Freshly ground black pepper

3 hard-boiled eggs (see page 23)

Snipped fresh dill, for sprinkling

In a large nonstick skillet, heat the olive oil over medium-high heat. Add the fresh beets and a generous pinch of salt and cook, stirring occasionally, until softened, about 5 minutes. Scrape into a large glass bowl and let cool for about 20 minutes.

Add the buttermilk, sour cream, pickled beets, cucumbers, and a generous pinch each of salt and pepper to the cooled shredded beets and mix well. Cover and refrigerate until the soup is chilled and bright pink, about 30 minutes. Stir in ½ cup water and season the soup generously with salt and pepper.

Ladle the soup into bowls and, using the small holes of a box grater, grate some hard-boiled egg on top (if you prefer, you can just chop the eggs and scatter them on top). Sprinkle snipped dill on top and serve cold.

DO IT AHEAD The soup can be refrigerated in an airtight container for up to 3 days.

NOTE I like to shred my beets in a food processor, but you can also do it on the large holes of a box grater.

TIP Dicing pickled beets is going to stain the heck out of any work surface, but I have a trick to prevent that. Wrap a big sheet of parchment paper around any small cutting board before slicing and dicing. The paper will stay intact as long as you don't slice too hard with the knife.

ALL-DAY
CASSOULET

HANDS-ON TIME
35 MIN

TOTAL TIME
7 TO 8 HRS ON
LOW OR 4 TO
5 HRS ON HIGH

SERVES 4

This dish came together one day when I was trying to clean out my freezer. I threw a bunch of meat (a random piece of pork shoulder, a half pack of sausage, some bacon) in my slow cooker, then added navy beans and a few other pantry staples. At first I called the recipe a stew. But then I changed the name to cassoulet because the combination of pork, sausage, and beans reminded me of that southern French classic—and also because it sounded way nicer.

4   thick-cut bacon slices, chopped

1   onion, finely chopped

4   garlic cloves, chopped

Kosher salt and freshly ground black pepper

1   quart low-sodium chicken broth

¾   pound dried navy beans (2 cups)

1   (15-ounce) can fire-roasted diced tomatoes

3   fresh thyme sprigs

2   dried bay leaves

½   pound smoked sausage, such as kielbasa or andouille, cut into 1-inch pieces

1   pound boneless pork shoulder, cut into 2-inch cubes

All-Purpose Lemony Bread Crumbs (page 281), for sprinkling

Finely chopped fresh parsley, for sprinkling

In a medium skillet, cook the bacon over medium heat, stirring occasionally, until just starting to render, about 3 minutes. Add the onion, garlic, and a generous pinch each of salt and pepper. Cook, stirring occasionally, until the onion is softened and the bacon is browned, about 7 minutes. Scrape the mixture into a slow cooker.

Add the broth to the slow cooker and then stir in the beans, tomatoes, thyme, bay leaves, 2 teaspoons salt, and ½ teaspoon pepper. Nestle the sausage and pork in the broth, pressing them down with a spoon to submerge. Cover and cook on Low for 7 to 8 hours or High for 4 to 5 hours, until the beans and pork are tender.

Spoon the cassoulet into bowls and serve, sprinkled with All-Purpose Lemony Bread Crumbs and finely chopped parsley.

LAMB & SWEET POTATO CURRY

HANDS-ON TIME
30 MIN

TOTAL TIME
7 TO 8 HRS ON
LOW OR 4 TO 5
HRS ON HIGH

SERVES 4

This is one of those slow-cooker recipes—super savory, with an edge of sweetness—that will make you happy you bought that machine in the first place. It's easy enough to throw together right before you leave the house, but you can save time in the morning by combining everything except the liquids in a big bowl and refrigerating overnight.

2 tablespoons unsalted butter

2 tablespoons peeled and minced fresh ginger

4 garlic cloves, minced

2 pounds well-trimmed boneless lamb shoulder, cut into 1½-inch pieces

1 pound sweet potatoes (2 medium), peeled and cut into 2-inch pieces

1½ tablespoons Madras curry powder

1 teaspoon turmeric powder

Kosher salt and freshly ground black pepper

1 (15-ounce) can unsweetened coconut milk

1 cup low-sodium chicken broth

Fresh cilantro, for sprinkling

Steamed rice, for serving

Lime wedges, for serving

In a small skillet, melt the butter over medium-high heat. Add the ginger and garlic and cook, stirring, until softened and lightly browned, about 3 minutes. Scrape into a large bowl. Add the lamb, sweet potatoes, curry powder, turmeric, 2 teaspoons salt, and 1 teaspoon pepper and toss well. Cover and refrigerate overnight (or, if you're doing this day-of, just mix it all in the insert of the slow cooker).

Transfer to a slow cooker and stir in the coconut milk and broth. Cover and cook on Low for 7 to 8 hours or High for 4 to 5 hours, until the lamb and sweet potatoes are tender. Season the curry with salt and pepper.

Ladle into bowls and sprinkle with cilantro. Serve with steamed rice and lime wedges.

DO IT AHEAD The curry can be refrigerated in an airtight container for up to 3 days. Reheat in a saucepan over medium heat, stirring occasionally, until hot.

SALADS & VEGETABLES

I'M NOT AFRAID TO ADMIT that I'm obsessed with salads and side dishes. In fact, when I eat out, I'm totally guilty of planning my entire meal around the starters and sides that grab my attention first. Get me in front of a buffet or hand me a big takeout menu and I *will* go to town, creating an entire meal out of salads and vegetables with no entrées to get in the way.

Because my love for these dishes is grand, I've spent way too much time over the years cooking them at home while the rest of my household not so patiently waits. These recipes always take longer to make than I think they will; ingredient lists tend to be unbearably long and prep times creep up and up and up. Blame the insane amount of chopping required.

But I refuse to give up! Instead, I've learned to follow two simple rules: select the biggest-bang-for-your-buck ingredients and use smart shortcuts. Here I share some of my favorite simple recipes, like Smashed Chickpea Salad Lettuce Wraps and Thai Beef Salad. Plus, I offer a few fresh ideas for healthily revamping indulgent favorites like Caesar salad. Because who wants to play the shame game?

BRUSSELS SPROUT, APPLE & PEAR
SLAW
112

GRILLED BROCCOLINI & ESCAROLE SALAD
with BBQ Sauce Vinaigrette
113

KRAB
Avocado & Grapefruit Salad
115

BEANS & PEAS
with Buttermilk Ranch
116

Smashed Chickpea Salad
LETTUCE WRAPS
119

THAI BEEF SALAD
with Peanuts
120

BLOODY MARY
PANZANELLA
121

BUTTON MUSHROOM
CARPACCIO
with Celery & Hazelnuts
122

Spicy Melon &
HEIRLOOM TOMATO SALAD
with Mozzarella
123

California-Style
FATTOUSH
127

Shaved Cauliflower & Radicchio
SALAD
with Yogurt Caesar
128

CRUSHED CUKES
with Chile-Lime Dressing
131

Quick-Braised
COLLARD GREENS
132

GOOD-LUCK PEAS
with Black Eyes
133

CAULIFLOWER
FRIED "RICE"
with Ginger & Soy
134

Rena's Sesame-Marinated
BROCCOLI
137

FINGERLINGS
with 40 Cloves of Garlic
138

SLOW-COOKED
GREEN BEANS
with Tomatoes & Bacon
140

Olive Oil & Herb
CRUSHED POTATOES
141

Extra-Crispy
POTATO STICKS
with Chipotle Mayo
144

MEXICAN-STYLE
STREET CORN
with Lime Mayo
147

Thai
SKILLET CORN
148

Brussels Sprout
& PEARL ONION HASH
with Burnt Almonds
149

Roasted Carrot & Avocado
PANZANELLA
150

BRUSSELS SPROUT, APPLE & PEAR SLAW

TOTAL TIME
20 MIN

SERVES 4

Coleslaw is one of the best things that could've ever happened to an American barbecue or block party. Not only am I a coleslaw fanboy, I happen to think of myself as a bit of a connoisseur. I make it year-round and in all forms. This version is one of my favorites because it takes coleslaw out of its summer context and gives it an autumnal feel thanks to the Brussels sprouts, apples, and pears.

⅓ cup mayonnaise

3 tablespoons apple cider vinegar

¾ teaspoon celery seeds

12 ounces Brussels sprouts, trimmed and thinly sliced

1 large Granny Smith apple, cored and julienned

1 very firm Bartlett pear, cored and julienned

Kosher salt and freshly ground black pepper

In a large bowl, whisk together the mayonnaise, vinegar, and celery seeds. Add the Brussels sprouts, apple, and pear and toss well. Season with salt and pepper and toss again. Serve.

TIP I prefer to slice Brussels sprouts by hand instead of using a food processor or mandoline because you can get them just thick enough that way, and I happen to love their just-firm-enough bite. To get long, thin slices that hold their natural shape, I slice them lengthwise. It's easy! Just trim the root so the sprout will stand on a work surface and slice down lengthwise. If you prefer, pick up store-bought sliced ones.

GRILLED BROCCOLINI & ESCAROLE SALAD

with BBQ Sauce Vinaigrette

TOTAL TIME
35 MIN

SERVES 4

It might surprise you to know I grill salad as often as I can, year-round, as long as I don't have to trek through snow or stand in a thunderstorm (I'm not afraid of rain, but lightning is another story—especially when I'm holding metal tongs). This salad is packed with two veggies that are totally grill-friendly. Broccolini and escarole hold up well over the fire and develop a slight smokiness that enhances their already bold flavors. I sometimes dress them in lemon juice and a showering of Parmesan, but I couldn't let you try this recipe without my BBQ Sauce Vinaigrette. Because: Grilling!

1   (1¼-pound) head escarole, dark outer leaves discarded

½   pound Broccolini, trimmed

3   tablespoons extra-virgin olive oil

Kosher salt and freshly ground black pepper

½   cup chopped fresh parsley

BBQ Sauce Vinaigrette (page 269), for serving

Fill a large bowl with water. Using a large knife, quarter the escarole lengthwise through the core. Holding each piece of escarole by the core, dip it in the water and swish it around to release any dirt. Shake out the excess water and put them cut-side down on paper towels to drain, then pat the outside dry with paper towels.

Light a grill or preheat a grill pan. On a large baking sheet, drizzle the Broccolini and escarole all over with the olive oil and season generously with salt and pepper. Grill the Broccolini and escarole over high heat, turning once, until lightly charred and crisp-tender, about 3 minutes for the escarole and 5 minutes for the Broccolini.

Cut the Broccolini and escarole into 2- to 3-inch pieces and transfer them to a platter. Scatter the parsley on top and drizzle with a little bit of the BBQ Sauce Vinaigrette. Serve right away, passing more vinaigrette at the table.

KRAB

AVOCADO & GRAPEFRUIT SALAD

HANDS-ON TIME
15 MIN

TOTAL TIME
20 MIN

SERVES 4

Okay, I know what you're thinking: *How did he misspell crab?* I didn't! I really truly mean krab, the super-tasty imitation crabmeat you may know best as the star of the California roll. It's made from real fish and sold in either the deli or fish section of your supermarket, so I think it's a great ingredient to play around with. Not to mention that it's inexpensive and easy to use (no picking through crab shells to extract the meat). This salad with juicy grapefruit, fruity olive oil, and creamy avocado will make you a krab konvert.

3   ruby red grapefruits

8   ounces krab (aka imitation crabmeat) chunks

2   Hass avocados, pitted, peeled, and cut into bite-size pieces

¼   cup extra-virgin olive oil

¼   cup minced fresh chives

Kosher salt and freshly ground black pepper

Using a knife, cut off the top and bottom ends of one grapefruit. Set the grapefruit on one of the cut sides to balance it and, working from the top to the bottom, cut off the peel and all of the bitter white pith. Working over a bowl, cut in between the membranes (the white lines that run vertically through the fruit) to release the sections and let them fall into the bowl. Squeeze the pulp that's left after you've cut out all the sections into a small bowl to release the juice; you should get about 3 tablespoons from the pulp of 1 grapefruit. Repeat with the remaining grapefruit. Reserve ¼ cup of the grapefruit juice and save the rest for another use (or drink it!).

On plates or a platter, layer the krab, grapefruit sections, and avocados. Drizzle with the grapefruit juice and olive oil. Sprinkle the chives on top, then season with salt and pepper and serve.

DO IT AHEAD   You can easily assemble this salad a few hours ahead. Add the juice, olive oil, chives, salt, and pepper just before serving to prevent the citrus from leaching its juices.

BEANS & PEAS

with Buttermilk Ranch

HANDS-ON TIME
25 MIN

TOTAL TIME
35 MIN

SERVES 4

Every summer I create at least one salad that becomes my go-to. One year this was it. It's the perfect sidekick for grilled steaks or lamb, but the ridiculously good buttermilk ranch makes this super-fresh salad satisfying on its own. All the crisp beans and peas get caught in the crunchy Boston lettuce, which entices you to eat with your hands. And not only do I condone that, I recommend it! Promise I won't tell.

Kosher salt

½ pound haricots verts or thin green beans

½ pound sugar snap peas, strings removed

1 cup fresh or thawed frozen peas (4 ounces)

½ cup buttermilk

½ cup mayonnaise

½ cup snipped fresh chives, plus 1 tablespoon minced

1 tablespoon minced fresh dill

¾ teaspoon garlic powder

¾ teaspoon onion powder

Freshly ground black pepper

1 small head Boston lettuce, cored and leaves torn

Fill a medium saucepan with water and bring to a boil over high heat, then add a generous pinch of salt. Fill a large bowl with ice and water. Add the haricots verts to the boiling water and cook until crisp-tender and bright green, 2 to 3 minutes. Using a slotted spoon, transfer to the ice bath to cool. Add the snap peas and peas to the boiling water and cook until crisp-tender and bright green, 1 to 2 minutes. Drain well and transfer to the ice bath to cool. Drain the beans and peas very well and then pat dry with paper towels, or give them a whirl in the salad spinner.

In a medium bowl, whisk together the buttermilk, mayonnaise, minced chives, dill, garlic powder, and onion powder. Season the ranch dressing generously with salt and pepper.

In a large serving bowl, toss the beans and peas with the lettuce, the snipped chives, and half the ranch. Season the salad with salt and pepper. Serve right away, passing additional ranch at the table.

DO IT AHEAD The cooked beans and peas can be covered with a damp paper towel and refrigerated overnight. The ranch can be refrigerated in an airtight container for up to 5 days.

SMASHED CHICKPEA SALAD
LETTUCE WRAPS

TOTAL TIME
20 MIN

SERVES 4 TO 6

I'm no vegetarian, but I sometimes find the limitations of meatless cooking to be inspiring. Consider this chickpea salad, which I created for a vegetarian friend who wanted his own version of a chicken salad. I've made it for myself ever since. It's just as satisfying as chicken salad and still offers a healthy dose of protein. Because I'm not interested in chasing down any runaway chickpeas (and I bet you aren't, either), I crush most of them so they hold the salad together just enough to eat it between slices of bread or in lettuce cups.

2	(15-ounce) cans chickpeas, drained and rinsed
2	medium celery ribs, minced
1/3	cup minced red onion
1/4	cup mayonnaise
3	tablespoons fresh lemon juice
	Kosher salt and freshly ground black pepper
1/4	cup snipped fresh chives
1/2	cup finely chopped fresh parsley
12	large Bibb or iceberg lettuce leaves, for serving

In a large bowl, using a potato masher or large whisk, coarsely smash most of the chickpeas (some of the chickpeas might still be whole, which is good).

Add the celery, onion, mayonnaise, and lemon juice to the chickpeas and mix well. Season generously with salt and pepper. Stir in the chives and parsley.

Spoon the chickpea salad into the lettuce leaves and serve.

DO IT AHEAD The chickpea salad can be refrigerated in an airtight container overnight. It's best if you stir in the chives and parsley just before serving, but it's no biggie if you can't.

THAI BEEF SALAD
with Peanuts

HANDS-ON TIME
20 MIN

TOTAL TIME
25 MIN

SERVES 4

I went through a phase of eating Thai beef salad every week for a year. I couldn't get enough of the version at a local restaurant near my apartment in Queens, which served the salad on a huge plate covered with shredded vegetables and mesclun. Sadly, the restaurant closed (life is hard in New York, people) and I vowed to develop my own recipe. It was then that I discovered green curry paste. Made with green chile, garlic, lemongrass, galangal (aka Thai ginger), and makrut lime, it's like an asteroid of flavor headed straight for your mouth. No joke, it's that good. Keep it on hand to make this salad and also to spike stir-fries and even chicken broth as a pick-me-up the next time you're under the weather.

1½	pounds flank steak or London broil, at room temperature
½	cup canola oil, plus more for brushing
	Kosher salt and freshly ground black pepper
⅓	cup fresh lime juice
3	tablespoons Thai green curry paste
5	ounces mixed baby lettuces
½	cup shredded carrot
½	cup honey-roasted peanuts, chopped
¼	cup thinly sliced red onion

Light a grill or preheat a grill pan.

Brush the steak with canola oil and season with salt and pepper. Grill over medium-high heat until lightly charred on the bottom, about 6 minutes. Flip the steak and grill until an instant-read thermometer inserted into the thickest part of the meat registers 125°F, 5 to 7 minutes longer. Transfer to a carving board and let rest for 5 minutes, then thinly slice across the grain.

Meanwhile, in a medium bowl, whisk together the lime juice, curry paste, and canola oil. Season the dressing with salt and pepper.

In a large bowl, toss the lettuces with the carrot and ¼ cup of the dressing. Transfer to plates and top with the steak, peanuts, and red onion. Serve, passing additional dressing at the table.

DO IT AHEAD   The dressing can be refrigerated in an airtight container for up to 5 days.

BLOODY MARY
PANZANELLA

HANDS-ON TIME
40 MIN

TOTAL TIME
55 MIN

SERVES 4

My husband, Jason, has a thing for Bloody Marys. This has inspired me to create all kinds of dishes with Bloody Mary flavors. Whether it's a dip, sauce, or salad, Jason's all over it. I'm happy to oblige, especially when it means I get to eat more salads. Here heirloom tomatoes mixed with horseradish, celery seeds, black pepper, Tabasco, and fresh celery deliver a virtual Bloody Mary experience. Oh, and before you even ask—yes, you can *totally* have an actual Bloody with it.

½ pound ciabatta bread, torn or cut into 1-inch pieces

⅓ cup extra-virgin olive oil

3 tablespoons fresh lemon juice

2 tablespoons freshly grated or drained prepared horseradish

1 tablespoon minced shallot

1 teaspoon freshly ground black pepper

¾ teaspoon celery seeds

1 small garlic clove, finely grated

½ teaspoon Tabasco or other Louisiana-style hot sauce

1¼ pounds ripe heirloom or vine-ripe tomatoes, cut into 1½-inch chunks

1 inner celery rib, thinly sliced

Kosher salt

1 cup celery leaves (or as many as you can pick from the top and inner parts of a celery bunch)

Preheat the oven to 375°F.

Spread the bread on a large rimmed baking sheet. Bake for 12 to 15 minutes, until lightly browned and slightly dry. Let cool.

Meanwhile, in a small bowl, whisk together the olive oil, lemon juice, horseradish, shallot, pepper, celery seeds, garlic, and Tabasco.

In a large serving bowl, toss the cooled bread with the tomatoes, celery, and horseradish dressing. Season with kosher salt and let stand for 10 minutes, stirring occasionally (you want the bread to start to soften but still have some bite to it). Stir in the celery leaves and serve.

DO IT AHEAD The toasted bread can be stored in an airtight container at room temperature for up to 5 days. The horseradish dressing can be refrigerated in an airtight container overnight.

BUTTON MUSHROOM
CARPACCIO

with Celery & Hazelnuts

HANDS-ON TIME
15 MIN

TOTAL TIME
30 MIN

SERVES 4

At the farmers' market in New York City, I once saw a giant morel that cost $60. You heard me: $60 for *one mushroom*. I'd take that money and buy six hundred white mushrooms (aka button mushrooms) instead. These underappreciated 'shrooms are flavorful and inexpensive, and when served raw, they're a terrific canvas for so many other flavors and textures.

½   cup hazelnuts

10   ounces white mushrooms, cleaned and very thinly sliced

½   cup lightly packed celery leaves

1   inner celery rib, cut into 1-inch matchsticks

3   tablespoons finely chopped fresh chives

⅓   cup extra-virgin olive oil

3   tablespoons fresh lemon juice

Kosher salt and freshly ground black pepper

Preheat the oven to 375°F.

Spread the hazelnuts in a pie plate or on a rimmed baking sheet. Bake for about 12 minutes, until the skins blister and the nuts are browned. Let the nuts cool slightly, then transfer to a clean kitchen towel. Fold the towel over the nuts and rub them together to remove the skins. Let the nuts cool completely, then finely chop.

Spread the sliced mushrooms on four plates or one large serving platter. Scatter the celery leaves and matchsticks, the chives, and the chopped hazelnuts over the mushrooms. Drizzle the olive oil and lemon juice on top and season generously with salt and pepper. Serve right away.

TIP   There's quite a bit of debate over whether to rinse mushrooms. I say—just do it! As long as you rinse them quickly, they shouldn't absorb much liquid. And even if they do, it sure beats cleaning each and every mushroom with a towel. I like to put the mushrooms in the basket of a salad spinner and rinse them under cold water to remove the dirt and debris, then spin them dry.

SPICY MELON & HEIRLOOM TOMATO SALAD

with Mozzarella

TOTAL TIME
30 MIN
SERVES 4

When I was a kid, my Nana Celia would plop me down on the sofa next to her and serve me half a cantaloupe showered with salt and pepper, transforming something that seemed so ordinary into an exotic, sophisticated dish. I used to feel so grown-up eating it, and I'll never, ever forget the impact it had on how I feel about these two essential seasonings. The update here, with its sweet and savory elements—melon, tomatoes, mozzarella, herbs—is my homage to Nana. I think she'd love this salad, and hopefully she'd be proud to find it in a book.

¼ cup extra-virgin olive oil

1½ tablespoons unseasoned rice vinegar

¼ cup minced red onion

¾ teaspoon Tabasco or other Louisiana-style hot sauce

Kosher salt and freshly ground black pepper

1 (3¼-pound) cantaloupe (see Note)

1 pound mixed heirloom tomatoes, halved if small and cut into chunks if large

8 ounces buffalo mozzarella cheese, torn or cut into 1-inch pieces

2 cups pita chips

1 cup lightly packed small fresh basil leaves

¼ cup snipped fresh dill

In a large serving bowl, whisk together the olive oil, vinegar, onion, and Tabasco. Season the dressing with salt and pepper.

On a work surface, using a large knife, cut the cantaloupe in half. Using a spoon, scoop out and discard the seeds. Put one half of the cantaloupe cut-side down on the work surface. Starting at the top and working down, cut off and discard the rind, then cut the melon into 1-inch pieces and add them to the large serving bowl (wrap the other half of the cantaloupe in plastic and refrigerate it for later—you only need half for this salad).

Add the tomatoes and mozzarella to the serving bowl and toss it all to coat. Fold in the pita chips, basil, and dill. Season the salad with salt and pepper and toss again. Serve right away.

NOTE If you'd rather not put the effort into peeling and cutting the cantaloupe at home, buy 12 ounces of cubed cantaloupe for this recipe.

Spicy Melon &
HEIRLOOM TOMATO SALAD
with Mozzarella

PAGE 123

CALIFORNIA-STYLE
FATTOUSH

TOTAL TIME
30 MIN

SERVES 4

When I was in high school in Stockton, California, my friends and I would jump into our cars and pop over to Podesto's for lunch. It was, I think, the fanciest grocery store in town, selling uncommon pasta shapes like orecchiette and bucatini as well as every kind of vegetable. The best part: their deli sandwiches. Because we were in a farming area with amazing produce everywhere, my favorite sandwich was as memorable for the vegetables (cucumber, alfalfa sprouts, tomatoes, and as much avocado as they'd give me) as for the hand-carved turkey and Dutch crunch bread. This fattoush—a classic Middle Eastern bread salad—was inspired by every sandwich Podesto's ever served me. I add storebought pita chips for the ease of it. The only thing that could make it better is Dutch crunch croutons. Maybe next time?

2 ears corn, husks and silks removed

⅓ cup extra-virgin olive oil

¼ cup champagne vinegar

2 tablespoons minced shallot

2 teaspoons Dijon mustard

Kosher salt and freshly ground black pepper

2 cups shredded cooked chicken (8 ounces)

12 ounces heirloom tomatoes, cut into 1-inch pieces

2 Persian cucumbers, cut into bite-size pieces

1 romaine heart, torn into bite-size pieces

3 cups pita chips (5 ounces)

1 Hass avocado, pitted, peeled, and cut into bite-size pieces

1 cup lightly packed sunflower sprouts

1 cup chopped fresh dill

1 cup chopped fresh cilantro

Roasted salted sunflower seeds, for sprinkling

Invert a small bowl and place it in the bottom of a large bowl. Working with one ear at a time, stand the corn on the small bowl and, using a knife, cut off the kernels so they fall into the large bowl. Remove the small bowl. You should have about 1 cup fresh kernels.

In a large serving bowl, whisk together the olive oil, vinegar, shallot, and mustard. Season the dressing with salt and pepper. Add the chicken, tomatoes, cucumbers, romaine, pita chips, avocado, sprouts, dill, and cilantro and toss well. Season generously with salt and pepper and toss again. Sprinkle with the sunflower seeds and serve right away.

SHAVED CAULIFLOWER & RADICCHIO SALAD

with Yogurt Caesar

TOTAL TIME
30 MIN

SERVES 4

This recipe was inspired by a raw-broccoli salad by cookbook goddess Deborah Madison. My friend Tina would serve it every year at her holiday party. She couldn't keep another friend of ours, Kate, and me from getting to it before she'd even finished tossing it. Still, she was such a good sport that she'd make a double batch and let us each take a container home. (I'm not sure about Kate, but I often finished my portion in the taxi.) For this version, I substitute raw cauliflower, which is packed with nutrients and has a wonderful crunchy texture. Cauliflower stands up well to strong flavors, so I love to toss it with an all-purpose yogurt Caesar dressing.

½ cup plain Greek yogurt

¼ cup champagne vinegar

¼ cup extra-virgin olive oil

2 tablespoons finely grated Parmesan cheese

1 tablespoon Dijon mustard

1 tablespoon anchovy paste or minced anchovies

2 garlic cloves, finely grated

½ teaspoon freshly ground black pepper

Kosher salt

1 (2-pound) head cauliflower, trimmed

4 ounces radicchio (½ head), sliced

1 (4- to 6-ounce) bunch watercress, trimmed of thick stems and chopped

In a large serving bowl, whisk together the yogurt, vinegar, olive oil, Parmesan, mustard, anchovy paste, garlic, and pepper. Season the dressing with salt.

Using a large knife, cut the cauliflower through the core into quarters. Thinly slice the quarters crosswise into thin shavings (it's okay if some of the florets start to crumble—it adds a lovely texture to the salad). Add all the cauliflower to the serving bowl along with the radicchio and watercress and toss to coat. Season with salt and toss again. Serve right away.

DO IT AHEAD The yogurt Caesar dressing can be refrigerated in an airtight container for up to 3 days.

CRUSHED CUKES

with Chile-Lime Dressing

TOTAL TIME
15 MIN

SERVES 4

Cucumbers are way more versatile than most people think—for instance, I adore them quickly sautéed with thin strips of pork. Even when it comes to salads, there are some new ideas to try. My favorite method is to lightly crush cucumber halves, then tear them into large chunks with my hands, Incredible Hulk–style. Not only is it super fun, but the pieces soak up the dressing better than thin slices would while remaining refreshing and crisp. So give this recipe a try—and give your knife a rest.

6   Persian cucumbers, rinsed and patted dry

2   tablespoons fresh lime juice

2   teaspoons canola or vegetable oil

2   teaspoons sambal oelek or other Asian chile sauce

1   teaspoon toasted sesame oil

1   cup small or torn large fresh basil leaves (use Thai basil, if you can find it!) (optional)

2   scallions, thinly sliced on an angle (optional)

    Kosher salt

On a work surface, cut the cucumbers in half crosswise. Work with one cucumber half at a time: Place a large knife flat on top of a cucumber half with the blade facing away from you and then lightly crush with your other hand. Repeat with the remaining cucumber halves, then tear the crushed cucumbers into chunks and transfer to a serving bowl.

In a small bowl, whisk together the lime juice, canola oil, sambal oelek, and sesame oil. Spoon the dressing over the crushed cucumber chunks and toss to coat. Fold in the basil and scallions and season with salt. Serve right away.

QUICK-BRAISED COLLARD GREENS

HANDS-ON TIME
30 MIN

TOTAL TIME
55 MIN

SERVES 6

Traditionally, collard greens are cooked for hours and hours, until they're insanely tender. I understand why people love the almost-silky texture, but I much prefer my collard greens to have a little bite. So when I cook them, I start by sautéing onion with bacon and garlic. Next (and here's the real trick) I add chicken broth, bring it to a simmer, and add the collard greens a handful at a time so they can wilt slightly. Once I have them all in the pot, I let them braise for just long enough to get nicely tender without becoming too soft. PS: The chicken broth adds lots of flavor, so don't substitute water.

2 tablespoons extra-virgin olive oil

1 medium red onion, finely chopped

2 thick-cut bacon slices, chopped

2 garlic cloves, thinly sliced

Kosher salt

1 (15-ounce) can low-sodium chicken broth

2¾ pounds collard greens, stemmed and chopped (see Tip)

2 tablespoons red wine vinegar, plus more for serving

Freshly ground black pepper

In a large saucepan, heat the olive oil over medium heat. Add the onion, bacon, garlic, and a generous pinch of salt and cook, stirring occasionally, until the onion is softened and the bacon fat is rendered, about 7 minutes.

Add the broth to the saucepan and bring to a boil over high heat. Add the collard greens in large handfuls, letting each handful wilt slightly before adding more. Cover and braise over medium-low heat, stirring occasionally, until the greens are just tender, 20 to 25 minutes. Stir in the vinegar and season the greens with salt and pepper. Transfer the greens to a serving bowl and serve, passing more vinegar at the table.

DO IT AHEAD The collard greens and their cooking liquid can be refrigerated in an airtight container overnight. Reheat in a saucepan over medium heat, stirring occasionally, until hot.

TIP If you prefer to buy your greens already stemmed and chopped, purchase about 1¼ pounds instead of the 2¾ pounds called for in the recipe.

GOOD-LUCK PEAS

with Black Eyes

HANDS-ON TIME
20 MIN

TOTAL TIME
1 HR 10 MIN

SERVES 6

For at least the past ten years, I've made black-eyed peas in some form for New Year's Eve, following a tradition of the American South that considers black-eyed peas to be good luck. Maybe I'm a little superstitious, but heck, why *not* follow a tradition that is so delicious? And if it happens to bring prosperity, then all the better. Some years, when I'm feeling lazy, I just mix a can of black-eyed peas into a big pot of collard greens. One year I transformed the peas into a spicy dip. But the herb-spiked version here is my favorite because it's tangy and fresh and can work as a main course alongside salad or cornbread. I much prefer dried beans here because they're one of the few dried legumes that don't require overnight soaking.

2	tablespoons extra-virgin olive oil
4	thick-cut bacon slices, chopped
1	pound dried black-eyed peas, picked over
1	quart low-sodium chicken broth
1	medium tomato, cut into 1-inch pieces
1	jalapeño, halved lengthwise
2	fresh cilantro sprigs, plus ½ cup chopped leaves
3	scallions, thinly sliced
¼	cup fresh lime juice
	Kosher salt and freshly ground black pepper

In a large saucepan, heat the olive oil over medium heat. Add the bacon and cook, stirring occasionally, until rendered but not crisp, about 5 minutes. Add the peas, broth, tomato, jalapeño, cilantro sprigs, and 3 cups water. Bring to a boil over high heat and then simmer over medium-low heat, stirring occasionally, until the beans are tender but not falling apart, 50 minutes to 1 hour (not all beans are created equal, so check them occasionally so you don't overcook them).

Pick out and discard the jalapeño and cilantro sprigs. Using a slotted spoon, transfer the peas and tomatoes to a serving bowl; discard the bean broth or reserve for another use. Fold in the chopped cilantro, the scallions, and lime juice. Season with salt and pepper. Serve hot, warm, or at room temperature (your choice).

DO IT AHEAD The cooked black-eyed peas can be refrigerated in an airtight container overnight. Bring them to room temperature before using.

CAULIFLOWER FRIED
"RICE"

with Ginger & Soy

TOTAL TIME
45 MIN

SERVES 4

If you've ever heard of a zoodle (translation: a zucchini noodle), then you already know that one way to cut back on carbs is to replace them with lookalike veggies. Allow me to introduce you to one of my favorites: cauliflower "rice." That's what you get when you shred cauliflower with a box grater. I stir-fry those faux grains with ginger and garlic, fold in lime juice, chile sauce, and other zesty flavorings, and end up with a guiltless version of a Chinese takeout favorite.

1 (2-pound) head cauliflower,
   leaves discarded
   (see Tip, page 136)

4 large eggs

   Kosher salt

4 tablespoons canola oil

1 small red onion, finely
   chopped

¼ cup peeled and minced
   fresh ginger

4 garlic cloves, minced

1 cup chopped fresh cilantro

4 large scallions, thinly sliced

¾ cup julienned or shredded
   carrot (see Tip, page 136)

3 tablespoons fresh lime
   juice

1 tablespoon low-sodium
   soy sauce

1 tablespoon sambal oelek
   or other Asian chile sauce

   Lime wedges, for serving

Quarter the cauliflower through the core. Hold a box grater firmly on a cutting board or in a large, shallow bowl. Holding one quarter of the cauliflower by the core, shred it on the large holes of the box grater in short movements until only the core is left in your hand; discard the core. The short movements form the best "rice," whereas long movements will create shreds that resemble flaked coconut. Repeat with the remaining cauliflower. Transfer the cauliflower "rice" to a medium bowl (you should have about 5 cups).

In another medium bowl, beat the eggs with a generous pinch of salt. In a large nonstick skillet, heat 1 tablespoon of the canola oil over medium-high heat. Add the egg and swirl it around the bottom of the pan. Let cook, undisturbed, until the bottom is very lightly browned and the egg is nearly cooked through (you'll see just a little bit of runny egg on top), 1 to 2 minutes. Using a rubber spatula, fold the egg over itself to form a half-moon. Let cook for 30 seconds, then slide it onto a work surface. Let the egg cool slightly, then cut it into ½-inch pieces.

RECIPE CONTINUES

In the same nonstick skillet, heat the remaining 3 tablespoons canola oil over high heat. Add the onion and cook, stirring, until just softened, about 3 minutes. Add the ginger and garlic and cook, stirring, until fragrant, 1 to 2 minutes. Add the cauliflower and cook, stirring, until just crisp-tender and hot, about 5 minutes. Stir in the eggs, cilantro, scallion, carrot, lime juice, soy sauce, and sambal oelek. Season generously with salt, transfer to bowls, and serve with lime wedges.

DO IT AHEAD   The uncooked cauliflower "rice" can be refrigerated in an airtight container for up to 3 days or frozen for up to 1 month.

TIPS   To julienne a carrot, slice it on an angle about ⅛ inch thick. Stack the slices on the cutting board and then cut them lengthwise into thick matchsticks. There you have it—julienned! It's easy enough, but if you'd rather not cut the carrot into julienne, you can shred it on the large holes of a box grater.

Many grocery stores sell cauliflower "rice" in the produce section. It can be a good shortcut when you're really pressed for time, but once you make your own there's no going back. You can also make cauliflower "rice" in the food processor by pulsing florets in batches.

RENA'S SESAME-MARINATED
BROCCOLI

HANDS-ON TIME
15 MIN

TOTAL TIME
30 MIN

SERVES 4

This is one of the easiest broccoli dishes I've ever made—fast, delicious, and a cinch to prep from the *Just Cook It!* pantry (simply add broccoli). I got the recipe from my late mother-in-law, Rena, who faxed over a copy of the handwritten card she stored in a Rolodex-style filing box in her kitchen. Even though I've memorized the recipe by now, I keep that fax to remind me of her and all the times she made it for me. The original recipe includes a note from her to "buy broccoli with a lot of little flowers." I'm sure that means "florets," and I think that's spot-on advice.

Kosher salt

2 pounds broccoli, cut into florets, stems peeled and sliced ¼ inch thick (see Tip)

¼ cup distilled white vinegar

¼ cup toasted sesame oil

1 tablespoon sugar

Toasted white and/or black sesame seeds, for sprinkling

Bring a large saucepan of water to a boil, and add a small handful of salt. Add the broccoli and cook until crisp-tender and bright green, about 3 minutes. Drain in a colander and cool under cold running water (this will stop the cooking). Drain again, then dry on paper towels or, for best results, spin dry in a salad spinner.

In a serving bowl, whisk together the vinegar, sesame oil, sugar, and ¾ teaspoon salt until the sugar and salt dissolve. Add the broccoli and toss to coat. Let stand for 15 minutes, then season with salt and sprinkle with toasted white and/or black sesame seeds. Serve at room temperature or slightly chilled.

DO IT AHEAD The marinated broccoli can be refrigerated in an airtight container overnight. Let stand at room temperature for 30 minutes before serving.

TIP Broccoli isn't exactly difficult to "butcher," but I have a trick that makes a lot of sense for cutting it into florets. I hold the broccoli with the florets down and the stem standing in the air. Using a knife, cut the florets off the stem, rotating the head as you go.

FINGERLINGS

with 40 Cloves of Garlic

HANDS-ON TIME
15 MIN

TOTAL TIME
45 MIN

SERVES 4

Okay, I admit there aren't actually forty cloves of garlic in this recipe. But for those of you who insist on counting, I will say that there are at least forty *pieces* of garlic because I start with big cloves—the biggest I can get from two heads—and cut them in half lengthwise. I'm hoping that after you've tried this recipe, you'll forgive me for exaggerating the number a little, because these crispy-creamy potatoes and garlic will rock your world. I serve them with just about anything, from my Flat-Roasted Chickens with Coriander & Lemon (page 212) to an everyday burger.

3 pounds fingerling potatoes, halved or quartered if large

1 lemon, thinly sliced and seeded

8 fresh thyme sprigs

3 small fresh rosemary sprigs

½ cup extra-virgin olive oil

Kosher salt and freshly ground black pepper

20 large garlic cloves, halved lengthwise

Preheat the oven to 450°F. Put a large rimmed baking sheet in the oven and let it preheat for 15 minutes (this will prevent the potatoes from sticking to the pan, and get them browning as quickly as possible).

In a large bowl, toss the potatoes, lemon, thyme, and rosemary with the olive oil and season generously with salt and pepper. Remove the preheated baking sheet from the oven and immediately spread the potato mixture in an even layer. Roast for about 15 minutes, until lightly browned. Scatter the garlic cloves evenly on top and, using a metal spatula, give the mixture a little stir. Roast for about 15 minutes more, until the potatoes and garlic are tender. Transfer to a platter and serve hot.

SLOW-COOKED
GREEN BEANS

with Tomatoes & Bacon

HANDS-ON TIME
20 MIN

TOTAL TIME
1 HR 5 MIN

SERVES 6

I really dig canned green beans. Are you with me? Perhaps I'm a little nuts, or maybe I'm just a bit nostalgic (I ate them so much growing up), but for me there's something so comforting about the tender texture. I challenge you to try my low-and-slow method for cooking green beans with bacon, tomatoes, and chicken broth; I'm pretty confident you'll remember when you loved the canned stuff, too.

6 bacon slices, chopped

2 tablespoons extra-virgin olive oil

1 red onion, finely chopped

4 garlic cloves, thinly sliced

Kosher salt and freshly ground black pepper

1½ pounds green beans, trimmed and cut into 1-inch lengths

1 (15-ounce) can diced tomatoes

1 (15-ounce) can low-sodium chicken broth

In a large saucepan, cook the bacon in the olive oil over medium heat, stirring occasionally, until just starting to brown, about 5 minutes. Add the onion, garlic, and a generous pinch each of salt and pepper. Cook, stirring occasionally, until the vegetables are softened and the bacon is browned, about 5 minutes. Add the green beans, tomatoes, and broth and bring to a boil over high heat. Simmer over low heat, stirring occasionally, until the beans are very tender, about 45 minutes. Season with salt and pepper and serve.

DO IT AHEAD Because these beans are already kind of soft, I have no problem refrigerating them overnight. Just warm them in a saucepan over medium heat before serving.

OLIVE OIL & HERB CRUSHED POTATOES

HANDS-ON TIME
25 MIN

TOTAL TIME
45 MIN

SERVES 4 TO 6

Once, when I was making my Fingerlings with 40 Cloves of Garlic (page 138) for houseguests, I accidentally overcooked the potatoes—a martini distracted me, my friends reported. Panic! But then I calmed down and started to improvise. I picked the potatoes up with my hands and tossed them into a serving bowl. They started to fall apart into chunks, so I figured I'd make some sort of warm salad. I drizzled a ridiculous amount of fruity olive oil all over them—this was key to its success—then folded in a ton of herbs. Delicious! The recipe has evolved slightly since that night, but every time I make it, I can't help but remember how it came to be. The lesson: Mistakes can often lead you to something far better. After all, when Julia Child couldn't flip her potato pancakes, she covered them with cream and cheese, threw them in the oven, and invented a new classic.

1½ pounds baby red potatoes

    Kosher salt

1 medium shallot, minced

½ teaspoon finely grated lemon zest

¼ cup fresh lemon juice

¾ cup extra-virgin olive oil

1 (2-ounce) bunch arugula, large stems discarded and leaves chopped

¾ cup chopped fresh parsley

½ cup snipped fresh dill

½ cup snipped fresh chives

    Freshly ground black pepper

Put the potatoes in a medium saucepan and add water to cover. Bring to a boil, add a generous pinch of salt, and simmer over medium heat until tender, 15 to 20 minutes. Drain and transfer them to a plate to cool slightly.

Meanwhile, in a large bowl, whisk together the shallot, lemon zest, and lemon juice; let stand for 5 minutes.

Using your fingers, lightly crush the potatoes and transfer to the large bowl. Add the olive oil and mix gently, then fold in the arugula, parsley, dill, and chives. Season generously with salt and pepper. Serve right away.

DO IT AHEAD If you're really looking to save a little time, you can prepare this recipe through the potato-crushing process and let it hang out at room temperature for a while. Add everything else just before serving; that way, the herbs stay fresh and green.

Olive Oil & Herb
CRUSHED POTATOES
PAGE 141

EXTRA-CRISPY
POTATO STICKS

with Chipotle Mayo

HANDS-ON TIME
20 MIN

TOTAL TIME
50 MIN

SERVES 4

One of my all-time favorite snacks is Potato Stix. You know the ones—those crispy matchsticks sold in indestructible tins providing the ultimate protection against breakage. I've always opted for the supersized container, which reminds me of the extra-tall Folgers coffee cans my grandma would use. The edge of the can would lightly scratch my forearm when I tried to reach the bottom for the crumbs. Ah, those glorious crumbs were everything to me.

Nowadays, I use Potato Stix to add crunch to everything from lobster rolls to salads. Sadly, they're becoming harder to find, so I've developed this recipe for extra-crispy potato sticks. They're not *quite* the same, but they do offer a fabulous crunch. And they're amazing dipped into chipotle mayo.

1 pound russet or other baking potatoes, scrubbed and patted dry

2 tablespoons extra-virgin olive oil

Kosher salt and freshly ground black pepper

½ cup mayonnaise

1 canned chipotle in adobo, seeded and minced, plus 1 tablespoon adobo sauce from the can

1 teaspoon fresh lime juice

Preheat the oven to 400°F. Place a large rimmed baking sheet in the center of the oven to preheat for at least 10 minutes.

Using a large sharp knife, cut a ¼-inch-thick slice off the bottom of each potato to keep them from rolling around. Cut the potatoes lengthwise into ¼-inch-thick slices. Stack the slices and then cut them lengthwise into ¼-inch-thick sticks.

In a large bowl, toss the potato sticks with the olive oil and season generously with salt and pepper. Remove the baking sheet from the oven and immediately add the potato sticks to it, spreading them in an even layer. Bake for about 30 minutes, until browned and crisp; stir the potato sticks halfway through baking.

Meanwhile, in a small bowl, whisk together the mayonnaise, chipotle, adobo sauce, and lime juice. Season the chipotle mayo with salt and pepper.

Serve the potato sticks with the chipotle mayo for dipping.

DO IT AHEAD The chipotle mayo can be refrigerated in an airtight container for up to 3 days.

MEXICAN-STYLE STREET CORN

with Lime Mayo

HANDS-ON TIME
15 MIN

TOTAL TIME
25 MIN

SERVES 4

I had my first Mexican-style corn in high school, thanks to my passion for flea markets. That's right: I was a seventeen-year-old boy who loved a rummage sale. My friend Brandon and I had ditched our classes to go to the open-air market in Galt. In between the fireworks stands and the stalls selling carved bald eagles were a scattering of food trailers—you heard me, kids, there were food trailers before there were food trucks. One served corn on the cob slathered in mayonnaise and sprinkled with chile-lime powder. It was shockingly good. It's hard to remember how many versions of street corn I tried over the years, but I'll never forget the one covered with cotija (fresh cheese) and cilantro because I had it the day I ran into a few teachers from my school who were taking a "sick" day, too.

4   ears corn

½   cup mayonnaise

1   teaspoon finely grated lime zest

1   tablespoon fresh lime juice

    Kosher salt and freshly ground black pepper

    Extra-virgin olive oil, for drizzling

½   cup finely chopped fresh cilantro

¼   cup freshly grated Parmesan cheese

    Mexican-style hot sauce, such as Cholula or Tapatío, for serving

Bring a large pot of salted water to a boil. Add the corn, still in their husks, and cook until just tender when pinched with tongs, about 5 minutes. If the corn is bobbing up out of the water, place a heatproof plate on top to keep them submerged. Using tongs, transfer the corn to a platter and let cool slightly, then pull back the husks and remove the silk. Tie the husks together with kitchen string.

Meanwhile, in a medium bowl, whisk together the mayonnaise, lime zest, and lime juice. Season the lime mayo with salt and pepper.

Light a grill. Drizzle the corn all over with olive oil. Grill over high heat, turning occasionally, until lightly charred in spots, about 5 minutes. Transfer to the platter. Spread the corn all over with the lime mayo and sprinkle with the chopped cilantro and Parmesan. Serve right away with hot sauce.

DO IT AHEAD   The lime mayo can be refrigerated in an airtight container for 3 days.

TIP   Boiling ears of corn in their husks makes them much easier to clean. Some people swear the cornhusks fall right off the ears if you microwave the corn for a couple of minutes, but my boiling method is even better.

THAI SKILLET CORN

HANDS-ON TIME
15 MIN

TOTAL TIME
30 MIN

SERVES 4 TO 6

I'm not sure if Thai flavors have ever found a foothold in the American South, but this recipe brings those two cultures together in the searing heat of a cast-iron skillet. The dish evokes classic Southern skillet corn, in which kernels are cooked in a pan until tender and charred; but I add lime juice, fish sauce, cilantro, and a few other Southeast Asian ingredients, plus shredded cooked chicken or poached shrimp if I want to turn it into a main course. If you've got crisp, sweet, height-of-summer corn, I humbly challenge you to find a better way to cook it.

6 ears corn, husks and silks removed

½ cup unsweetened coconut flakes or chips

3 tablespoons fresh lime juice

1 tablespoon Asian fish sauce

1 tablespoon packed light brown sugar

2 tablespoons canola or vegetable oil

1 cup chopped fresh cilantro

2 scallions, thinly sliced

1 fresh hot red chile, thinly sliced

Kosher salt and freshly ground black pepper

Invert a small bowl and place it in the bottom of a large bowl. Working with one ear at a time, stand the corn on the small bowl and, using a knife, cut off the kernels so they fall into the large bowl. Remove the small bowl. You should have about 3½ cups fresh kernels.

In a large cast-iron skillet, toast the coconut over medium heat, stirring, until lightly browned, 3 to 5 minutes. Transfer to a plate to cool. In a small bowl, whisk together the lime juice, fish sauce, and brown sugar.

Heat the same skillet over medium-high heat. Add the canola oil and swirl to coat the pan. Add the corn kernels and cook, stirring occasionally, until the corn is crisp-tender, about 5 minutes. Remove from the heat and stir in the lime mixture, cilantro, scallions, and red chile. Season the corn lightly with salt and pepper. Sprinkle with the toasted coconut and serve hot from the skillet.

BRUSSELS SPROUT & PEARL ONION HASH

with Burnt Almonds

HANDS-ON TIME
25 MIN

TOTAL TIME
40 MIN

SERVES 4 TO 6

Have I told you already how much I love Brussels sprouts? Probably. But let me put in a plug for pearl onions, too. I think most of us have only ever had the frozen ones, possibly at a grandmother's house, probably not by choice. Totally old school. I'm not going to lie: I love frozen pearl onions. But for the recipe below, I highly recommend using fresh ones because their texture can't be beat. When shopping, look for the red ones—they're my favorite—and try to buy them peeled if you can. If not, this recipe has a tip for peeling them pretty easily.

¼ cup extra-virgin olive oil

½ cup whole almonds (with or without their skins)

2 tablespoons unsalted butter

1 pound Brussels sprouts, halved if small, quartered if large

½ pound red or white pearl onions, peeled (see Tip)

3 fresh thyme sprigs

Kosher salt and freshly ground black pepper

¼ cup finely chopped fresh parsley

2 tablespoons fresh lemon juice

Preheat the oven to 425°F.

In a large skillet, heat the olive oil over medium heat until shimmering. Add the almonds and cook, stirring occasionally, until deeply browned and fragrant, about 5 minutes. Using a slotted spoon, transfer the almonds to a paper towel–lined plate to drain and cool, then coarsely chop. Leave the oil in the skillet.

In the same skillet, melt the butter in the reserved oil over medium-high heat. Add the Brussels sprouts and cook, undisturbed, until browned on the bottom, about 5 minutes. Add the onions, thyme sprigs, and a generous pinch each of salt and pepper. Cook, stirring occasionally, until everything is coated in the oil and sizzling, about 2 minutes. Transfer the skillet to the oven and bake until the Brussels sprouts and onions are tender, about 15 minutes. Stir in the parsley and lemon juice, then season with salt and pepper. Serve hot.

TIP Trim off just the root end of the pearl onions. Fill a large bowl with ice water. Bring a medium saucepan of water to a boil. Add the onions and blanch them until the skins just start to wrinkle, 30 seconds to 1 minute. Using a slotted spoon, transfer the onions to the ice water to cool, then pinch them out of their skins.

ROASTED CARROT & AVOCADO
PANZANELLA

HANDS-ON TIME
35 MIN

TOTAL TIME
1 HR 15 MIN

SERVES 8 TO 10

A while back, my buddy Jesse Tyler Ferguson, the incredibly talented actor best known for his role on *Modern Family*, started a food blog with his friend Julie Tanous. It's filled with healthy riffs on classic recipes—lots of Paleo, lots of gluten-free. All delicious! To celebrate the launch, our mutual friend Ellen Bennett, an apron designer, threw a potluck brunch at her place in LA, so I flew out. Jesse and I woke up early that morning and each prepared something to bring. He made a tangy-fresh salad with fresh and pickled tomatoes. Me? I made this recipe. Roasted-carrot salads aren't anything new, but I definitely amped mine up.

1	pound sourdough bread, cut or torn into bite-size pieces
¾	cup extra-virgin olive oil
	Kosher salt and freshly ground black pepper
1½	pounds small mixed-color carrots, halved lengthwise
1	tablespoon coriander seeds, crushed
2	teaspoons cumin seeds
1	orange, cut into wedges
1	lemon, halved
⅓	cup champagne vinegar
1	shallot, minced
1½	tablespoons Dijon mustard
4	ripe but firm Hass avocados, pitted, peeled, and cut into wedges
4	cups watercress, thick stems removed

Preheat the oven to 400°F.

On a large rimmed baking sheet, toss the bread with ¼ cup of the olive oil and season generously with salt and pepper. Spread in an even layer and bake for about 12 minutes, until golden and almost crisp. Transfer to a bowl and let cool. Keep the oven on.

Meanwhile, in a large bowl, toss the carrots, 2 tablespoons of the olive oil, and the coriander and cumin seeds. Squeeze the orange and lemon over the carrots, then add the squeezed fruit to the bowl, too. Season generously with salt and pepper and toss to mix. Spread on two large rimmed baking sheets and roast for 20 to 25 minutes, until lightly charred and tender. Let cool; discard the orange and lemon.

In a small bowl, whisk together the vinegar, shallot, mustard, and the remaining 6 tablespoons olive oil. Season the vinaigrette with salt and pepper.

On a large serving platter or in a serving bowl, gently toss the bread, carrots, and avocados with the vinaigrette. Add the watercress, season with salt and pepper, and toss to mix. Serve at room temperature.

PASTA & GRAINS

PASTA RECIPES ALWAYS SOUND SO SIMPLE, but the ones we love the most can be so frustrating. I know that I experimented and failed with these dishes as soon as I decided to get serious about cooking. When I attempted my first lasagna, for instance, I followed a classic recipe (the source of which shall remain nameless) and spent hours carefully preparing my ingredients and meticulously constructing the layers before sliding the whole thing in the oven. It looked like perfection, but when it emerged two hours later, it was literally a hot mess. Another time I attempted carbonara with similar results, though this hot mess was filled with scrambled eggs.

I didn't grow up in an Italian-American family—our version of lasagna was shepherd's pie—but over time I've become a lot more confident in my abilities. I've even figured out a few shortcuts to make life easier. So, in honor of my first lasagna—and yours, too—this chapter is filled with no-fail recipes. Plus, you'll find other dishes featuring rice, quinoa, and bulgur. All feature my favorite technique: cooking the grains in a large pot of water, as if boiling pasta.

BUCATINI

with Freshest Tomato Sauce

154

Slow-Cooker
TURKEY MEATBALLS

with Spaghetti

155

GRANDMA'S
CHILI MAC

157

RAVIOLI
LASAGNA
WITH ARUGULA

158

Couscous
PAELLA

with Chicken & Andouille

163

MEXICAN-STYLE
SOPITA

with Farmer Cheese

164

FREEKEH & HARICOTS VERTS

with Baby Kale & Preserved Lemon

165

FIDEOS

with Lamb Sausage, Chickpeas & Mint

166

Foolproof Pasta
CARBONARA

with Radicchio

169

No-Stir
RISOTTO

with Shrimp & Clams

170

RICOTTA
GNUDI

with Spinach & Dukka

173

Rice & Pork
CONGEE

with Chiles, Crispy Garlic & Ginger

175

Quinoa
BURGERS

with Avocado Mayo & Pea Shoots

176

HEATHER'S
RED RICE

178

STOVETOP
MAC 'N' CHEESE

with Bacon Bread Crumbs

179

Quinoa-Pork
LARB

181

BUCATINI

with Freshest Tomato Sauce

HANDS-ON TIME
20 MIN

TOTAL TIME
30 MIN

SERVES 4

I made a bargain with myself, dear reader, that I'd only beg you once in this book. So here I go: Please, please, *please* don't be fooled by the simplicity of this recipe. I know what you're thinking—it seems so boring! But the sauce, made with super-fresh summer tomatoes, is intensely flavorful but light enough to still let the pasta make an impression. So give this recipe a whirl and then hit me up on social @justinchapple with your thoughts.

Kosher salt

1¼ pounds ripe tomatoes (about 4 medium), halved crosswise

1 pound bucatini pasta

¼ cup extra-virgin olive oil, plus more for drizzling

2 tablespoons unsalted butter

¼ teaspoon red pepper flakes

Freshly ground black pepper

¼ cup finely grated Parmesan cheese, plus more for sprinkling

Bring a large pot of water to a boil, and add a small handful of salt.

Working over a bowl, grate the cut side of the tomato halves on the large holes of a box grater until only the skin remains in your hand; discard the skins.

Cook the bucatini in the boiling water according to the package directions until al dente, 8 to 10 minutes. Reserve 1 cup of the cooking water, then drain the pasta.

In the same large pot, combine the grated tomato with the olive oil, butter, red pepper flakes, 2 teaspoons black pepper, ½ teaspoon salt, and ½ cup of the reserved cooking water. Bring to a boil over medium-high heat. Add the pasta and cook, stirring vigorously, until the pasta is coated in a light sauce, about 3 minutes. Stir in the Parmesan and season with salt and black pepper. Transfer the pasta to bowls. Drizzle with olive oil and sprinkle with black pepper and Parmesan. Serve right away.

SLOW-COOKER TURKEY MEATBALLS

with Spaghetti

HANDS-ON TIME
30 MIN

TOTAL TIME
7 TO 8 HRS ON
LOW OR 4 TO 5
HRS ON HIGH

SERVES 4

Here's the thing about meatballs: They're not difficult to make. Unfortunately, they splatter everywhere when you pan-fry them and they are too labor-intensive for a weeknight (unless you're making the version on page 229). With this recipe, I've solved both problems by using a slow cooker, so now you can keep your stove clean *and* eat spaghetti and meatballs on a Monday.

1   pound ground turkey, preferably dark meat

1   small onion, half minced and half left intact

¾   cup plain dry bread crumbs

½   cup finely grated Parmesan cheese, plus more for sprinkling

½   cup finely chopped fresh parsley

⅓   cup whole milk

1   large egg

3   garlic cloves, minced

1   teaspoon freshly ground black pepper

Kosher salt

3   cups good-quality marinara sauce, such as Rao's

1   fresh basil sprig

1   pound spaghetti

In a large bowl, combine the turkey, minced onion, bread crumbs, Parmesan, parsley, milk, egg, garlic, pepper, and 2 teaspoons of salt and mix well. Form the mixture into 16 meatballs.

Put the marinara sauce in a slow cooker. Nestle the meatballs, the onion half, and the basil sprig in the sauce. Cover and cook on Low for 7 to 8 hours or on High for 4 to 5 hours, until the meatballs are cooked through and tender. Discard the onion half and the basil sprig.

Bring a large pot of water to a boil, and add a small handful of salt. Cook the spaghetti in the boiling water according to the package directions until al dente, 10 to 12 minutes. Drain the pasta and transfer to shallow bowls or a serving platter. Spoon the meatballs and sauce on the spaghetti. Sprinkle with Parmesan and serve.

DO IT AHEAD   The meatballs and sauce can be refrigerated in an airtight container overnight. Reheat gently in a large saucepan over medium-low heat.

GRANDMA'S
CHILI MAC

HANDS-ON TIME
35 MIN

TOTAL TIME
55 MIN

SERVES 6

This recipe honors a touchstone of my youth: boxed mac and cheese. Grandma Barbara would add sautéed onions, ground beef, canned tomatoes, and chili powder to produce an inexpensive and very tasty stovetop dinner in 15 minutes flat. I make my version completely from scratch, but it's still packed with the same bold flavors. Grandma didn't bake hers and you don't have to bake mine, either (just cook the mixture over low heat until the cheese has melted), but you will miss the crunchy panko topping, which is one of my favorite parts.

1 pound elbow macaroni or other small pasta shape

   Kosher salt

1 tablespoon extra-virgin olive oil, plus more for drizzling

1 large onion, finely chopped

1 large garlic clove

1 jalapeño, seeded and minced

1 pound ground beef

1 tablespoon all-purpose flour

1 tablespoon chili powder

1 (15-ounce) can diced tomatoes

1 cup half-and-half

2 cups shredded sharp cheddar cheese

1 cup finely chopped scallions, plus more for sprinkling

   Freshly ground black pepper

1½ cups panko bread crumbs

Preheat the oven to 400°F.

Bring a large pot of water to a boil, and add a small handful of salt. Cook the pasta in the boiling water according to the package directions until al dente, 7 to 9 minutes. Drain well, then drizzle with olive oil (just a little to prevent sticking) and toss to coat.

In the same pot, heat the olive oil over medium-high heat. Add the onion, garlic, jalapeño, and a generous pinch of salt. Cook, stirring occasionally, until the vegetables are softened, about 7 minutes. Add the beef and cook, breaking the meat up with a spoon, until just cooked through, about 7 minutes. Stir in the flour and chili powder until evenly coated, then stir in the tomatoes and half-and-half and simmer until thickened slightly, 3 to 5 minutes. Remove the pot from the heat and stir in the pasta, cheese, and scallions. Season the pasta mixture with salt and pepper.

Scrape the pasta mixture into six 8-ounce baking crocks or a 2-quart baking dish. In a medium bowl, mix the panko with a generous drizzle of olive oil, then sprinkle it on top of the pasta. Bake for about 20 minutes, until bubbling and the top is golden.

Sprinkle with thinly sliced scallions and serve hot.

RAVIOLI LASAGNA

with Arugula

HANDS-ON TIME
20 MIN

TOTAL TIME
1 HR 15 MIN

SERVES 6 TO 8

This is definitely not a traditional lasagna, but who cares when you can make such a good, fast approximation on a weeknight? Store-bought cheese ravioli are the ultimate hack because they let you skip all the layering and spreading. Just parboil them, tear up some fresh mozzarella, and open a jar of good marinara sauce. I sauté the sauce quickly with some ground beef for a cheater Bolognese, but you can skip that step entirely for a veggie version.

2	tablespoons extra-virgin olive oil
1	pound lean ground beef
	Kosher salt and freshly ground black pepper
3	cups good-quality marinara sauce, such as Rao's
1	teaspoon red pepper flakes
3¼	pounds prepared cheese ravioli, thawed if frozen
2	cups packed chopped baby arugula, plus leaves for sprinkling
1	pound fresh mozzarella cheese, sliced ¼ inch thick and torn into pieces

Preheat the oven to 400°F.

In a large skillet, heat the olive oil over medium heat until shimmering. Add the beef and a generous pinch each of salt and black pepper and cook, breaking up the meat with a wooden spoon, until just cooked through, about 7 minutes. Stir in the marinara sauce and red pepper flakes and cook, stirring occasionally, until bubbling, about 5 minutes. Season the sauce with salt and black pepper.

Spread 1 cup of the sauce over the bottom of a 9 by 13-inch ceramic baking dish and arrange half the ravioli on top. Spread half the remaining sauce on the ravioli and sprinkle the arugula on top. Scatter half the mozzarella on the arugula and season with salt and black pepper. Layer the remaining ravioli, sauce, and cheese on top.

Cover the lasagna tightly with aluminum foil and bake for about 30 minutes, until the filling is bubbling and the cheese has melted. Uncover the lasagna and bake for 15 minutes more, until the top is lightly browned. Let stand for 10 minutes, then sprinkle with arugula and serve.

DO IT AHEAD   The unbaked layered lasagna can be covered and refrigerated overnight. Bring it to room temperature and then bake it as directed in step 4.

RECIPE CONTINUES

Simmer ground beef in marinara sauce.

Spread 1 cup of sauce in the baking dish and arrange half the ravioli on top.

RAVIOLI
LASAGNA
with Arugula
PREP

Top with half the remaining sauce.

Top with half the cheese and all of the arugula.

Arrange the remaining ravioli on top.

Finish the layering with the remaining sauce and cheese, then bake.

COUSCOUS
PAELLA

with Chicken & Andouille

HANDS-ON TIME
35 MIN

TOTAL TIME
1 HR

SERVES 4

My greatest fear when making paella is under- or overcooking the rice. So I've started using a substitute—couscous. I know what you're thinking: If there's no rice, it's not paella! You're right, it's not. But once you learn how easy couscous is to work with, you might just start using it in all kinds of recipes that call for rice.

2 tablespoons extra-virgin olive oil

4 whole chicken legs (2 pounds)

Kosher salt and freshly ground black pepper

6 ounces andouille sausage, sliced

1 onion, finely chopped

1 jalapeño, seeded and minced

3 large garlic cloves, minced

½ cup dry white wine

1 cup low-sodium chicken broth

½ cup tomato sauce

1 small pinch of saffron threads

1½ cups couscous

1 medium tomato, finely diced

1 cup frozen peas (4 ounces)

Chopped fresh parsley, for sprinkling

Hot sauce, for serving

Preheat the oven to 425°F.

In a large deep skillet, heat the olive oil over medium heat. Season the chicken legs all over with salt and pepper. Add the chicken legs to the skillet skin-side down and cook until the skin is browned and crisp, about 7 minutes. Flip the chicken legs and scatter the sausage around them. Transfer to the oven and roast for 15 to 20 minutes, until an instant-read thermometer inserted into the thickest part of each piece of chicken registers 160°F. Transfer the chicken legs and sausage to a plate. Keep the oven on.

Add the onion, jalapeño, garlic, and a generous pinch of salt to the skillet. Cook over medium heat, stirring occasionally, until the onion is softened, about 5 minutes. Stir in the wine and simmer until almost evaporated, 2 to 3 minutes. Stir in the broth, tomato sauce, and saffron and bring to a boil over high heat. Stir in the couscous, tomato, and peas. Nestle the chicken and sausage in the couscous, cover the skillet, and roast in the oven for about 10 minutes, until the couscous is tender and the liquid has been absorbed.

Sprinkle with parsley and serve with hot sauce.

MEXICAN-STYLE SOPITA

with Farmer Cheese

HANDS-ON TIME
20 MIN

TOTAL TIME
30 MIN

SERVES 4

I lived with my best friend Brandon during my first year in New York City. We shared a two-bedroom, railroad-style apartment in Queens, where we pretty much spent every cent we had on rent (and the occasional $5 bottle of wine). This was Brandon's version of Top Ramen because it was super cheap and still exceptionally satisfying. The trick is to toast pasta shells in butter and oil. It really is a brilliant technique because it adds a particularly delicious nutty flavor—much like you get from browned butter—as well as a toothsome texture.

3 tablespoons unsalted butter

3 tablespoons extra-virgin olive oil

½ pound small pasta shells

1 onion, finely chopped

1 jalapeño, seeded and minced

2 garlic cloves, minced

Kosher salt

1 quart low-sodium chicken broth

1 (8-ounce) can tomato sauce

Freshly ground black pepper

Sliced radishes, for topping

Fresh cilantro leaves, for topping

Crumbled farmer cheese, for topping

In a large saucepan, melt the butter in the olive oil over medium-high heat. Add the pasta and cook, stirring, until the pasta is lightly browned, about 8 minutes. Add the onion, jalapeño, garlic, and a generous pinch of salt. Cook over medium heat, stirring occasionally, until the onion is softened, 5 to 7 minutes. Stir in the broth, tomato sauce, and 2 cups water. Simmer over medium-high heat, stirring occasionally, until the pasta is tender and coated in a light sauce, about 10 minutes. Season the sopita with salt and pepper.

Spoon the sopita into bowls and top with sliced radishes, cilantro leaves, and crumbled farmer cheese.

FREEKEH & HARICOTS VERTS

with Baby Kale & Preserved Lemon

HANDS-ON TIME
20 MIN

TOTAL TIME
1 HR 10 MIN

SERVES 4

Recently I was poking around in my pantry and came across a bag of freekeh, a Middle Eastern grain that's finally coming to more grocers in the United States. It sounds exotic but it's actually just green wheat, roasted to intensify the taste, and it's very nutritious and versatile. Is it the next farro? I have no idea. But I do know it's a great canvas for other flavors, as with the green beans and preserved lemons here.

Kosher salt

½ pound haricots verts or thin green beans, trimmed and halved crosswise

1 cup freekeh

¼ cup extra-virgin olive oil

3 tablespoons champagne vinegar

2 tablespoons minced Speedy Preserved Lemons (page 267) or store-bought preserved lemon

Freshly ground black pepper

3 cups lightly packed baby kale (2 ounces)

Chopped roasted almonds, for sprinkling (optional)

Bring a large saucepan of water to a boil, and add a generous pinch of salt. Fill a medium bowl with ice and water.

Add the haricots verts to the boiling water and cook until crisp-tender, about 3 minutes. Using a slotted spoon, transfer to the ice water to cool. Drain well, then pat dry with paper towels.

Cook the freekeh over medium-high heat in the boiling water, stirring occasionally, until tender, 15 to 20 minutes. Drain well in a fine sieve and then return to the hot saucepan. Cover and let steam for 10 minutes, then fluff with a fork and spread on a large plate to cool.

Meanwhile, in a serving bowl, whisk together the olive oil, vinegar, and preserved lemons. Season the dressing with salt and pepper. Add the haricots verts, cooled freekeh, and baby kale and toss well. Season with salt and pepper and toss again. Sprinkle with chopped toasted almonds and serve.

FIDEOS

with Lamb Sausage, Chickpeas & Mint

TOTAL TIME
45 MIN

SERVES 4

Fideos are thin noodles used in a paella-like Spanish dish called *fideuà*. My variation follows the classic method of sautéing angel hair pasta in a skillet to add a toasty flavor. I love this dish, but I won't lie—I sometimes skip the pasta and double the chickpeas to make a fast Mediterranean-style stew. After all, we're just cooking, not performing surgery.

2 tablespoons unsalted butter

12 ounces angel hair pasta, broken

1 tablespoon extra-virgin olive oil

½ pound merguez sausage, casings removed and meat crumbled

1 medium red onion

4 garlic cloves

½ teaspoon red pepper flakes

3 cups low-sodium chicken broth

1 (8-ounce) can tomato sauce

1 (15-ounce) can chickpeas, drained and rinsed

Crumbled farmer cheese, for topping

Plain Greek yogurt, for serving

Fresh mint leaves, for topping

In a large saucepan, melt the butter over medium heat. Add the broken pasta and cook, stirring frequently, until golden all over, about 7 minutes. Transfer the pasta to a large bowl.

In the same large saucepan, heat the olive oil over medium-high heat. Add the merguez and cook, stirring occasionally, until browned, about 5 minutes. Add the onion, garlic, and red pepper flakes and cook, stirring, until just softened, about 5 minutes. Stir in the broth and tomato sauce and bring to a boil. Stir in the toasted pasta and chickpeas and simmer over medium-high heat, stirring continuously, until the pasta is al dente and coated in a thick sauce, 5 to 7 minutes.

Ladle the noodles into shallow bowls and top with crumbled farmer cheese, Greek yogurt, and mint leaves. Serve immediately.

FOOLPROOF PASTA CARBONARA

with Radicchio

HANDS-ON TIME
25 MIN

TOTAL TIME
35 MIN

SERVES 4

After many failed attempts (I'm guessing there was wine involved . . . okay, there was *definitely* wine involved), I've finally figured out how to make an excellent carbonara. To keep the eggs from scrambling, I temper them with some of the cooking water before adding the hot pasta. Be sure your cooking water is hot, even if you need to pop it in the microwave, because that'll "cook" your eggs just enough.

Kosher salt

1 pound spaghetti

¼ cup extra-virgin olive oil, plus more for drizzling

6 large egg yolks

¾ cup finely grated Parmesan cheese, plus more for sprinkling

Freshly ground black pepper

6 ounces thick-cut pancetta, bacon, or salami, finely diced

½ head radicchio, cored and cut into 1-inch pieces

2 garlic cloves, thinly sliced

1 teaspoon red pepper flakes

⅓ cup chopped fresh chives

Bring a large pot of water to a boil, and add a small handful of salt. Cook the pasta in the boiling water according to the package directions until al dente, 10 to 12 minutes. Scoop out 1½ cups of the cooking water, then drain the pasta in a colander and toss it with a light drizzle of olive oil to keep it from sticking.

In a medium bowl, whisk together the egg yolks, Parmesan, 1 teaspoon black pepper, and a pinch of salt. Very gradually whisk in the reserved pasta water until smooth. (The reserved water should be hot, so heat it in the microwave if it's not. It's the hot water that'll cook the egg yolks so you don't accidentally scramble them when trying to do it in the pot.)

Meanwhile, in the same large pot, heat ¼ cup of the olive oil over medium heat. Add the pancetta and cook, stirring, until browned and almost crisp, about 5 minutes. Add the radicchio, garlic, and red pepper flakes and cook, stirring, until the radicchio just starts to wilt, about 3 minutes. Add the spaghetti and cook, tossing, until hot and coated in the fat, about 2 minutes. Remove from the heat, add the egg mixture, and toss vigorously until the pasta is coated in a creamy sauce, about 2 minutes. Stir in the chives and season with salt and black pepper.

Transfer the carbonara to shallow bowls, sprinkle with grated Parmesan, and serve hot.

NO-STIR RISOTTO

with Shrimp & Clams

HANDS-ON TIME
30 MIN

TOTAL TIME
1 HR 5 MIN

SERVES 4

My sister-in-law, Melissa, is a die-hard risotto fan. She is always busy running around after her two little girls, Bree and Maddie, so I feel like it must be calming for her to stand still and focus on one thing for an extended period of time. I can't find that same sort of Zen. Anyone who knows me knows that I'm a little (ahem, *very!*) impatient. I like fast results that satisfy my need for immediate gratification. That's why I created this no-stir take on risotto that lets me gather my ingredients and compose a salad while the rice cooks.

¼ cup extra-virgin olive oil, plus more for drizzling

1 large onion, finely chopped

Kosher salt and freshly ground black pepper

1 (16-ounce) package Arborio rice (2½ cups)

¾ cup dry white wine

7 cups low-sodium chicken broth

1 cup grated Parmesan cheese

2 teaspoons finely grated lemon zest

1 tablespoon fresh lemon juice

20 medium shrimp, peeled and deveined

20 small littleneck clams, scrubbed

Chopped fresh parsley or tarragon, for sprinkling

Preheat the oven to 350°F.

In a large enameled cast-iron casserole or a Dutch oven, heat the olive oil over medium heat until shimmering. Add the onion and a generous pinch each of salt and pepper. Cook, stirring occasionally, until softened but not browned, about 7 minutes. Add the rice and cook, stirring, until translucent, about 2 minutes. Add the wine and simmer until evaporated, about 2 minutes. Add 5 cups of the chicken broth and bring to a boil over high heat. Cover the casserole and bake in the oven for about 20 minutes, until the rice is tender and the broth has been absorbed.

Add the Parmesan, lemon zest, lemon juice, and the remaining 2 cups broth to the rice. Stir vigorously until creamy, about 2 minutes. Season the risotto with salt and pepper. Nestle the shrimp and clams evenly in the rice, cover, and bake for 15 to 20 minutes more, until the shrimp are pink and the clams open; discard any clams that do not open. Drizzle with olive oil and sprinkle chopped parsley or tarragon on top. Serve right away.

RICOTTA
GNUDI

with Spinach & Dukka

HANDS-ON TIME
30 MIN

TOTAL TIME
45 MIN

SERVES 4

I'm gonna guess that the *nonnas* don't make their pasta with a food processor and an ice cream scoop. But when it comes to the gnocchi-like dumplings called gnudi, I'm all about finding a shortcut (clearly!). The old-school method is to very gently shape the gnudi into perfect little ovals on a floured work surface, but I'm happy to scoop balls of dough right from the food processor and drop them directly into a pot of simmering water. These gnudi are big, fluffy pillows of creamy ricotta, the kind you'd find at one of my favorite New York City restaurants, The Spotted Pig. The sprinkling of dukka, an Egyptian seed-and-nut mix, really makes the dish.

2   cups whole-milk ricotta cheese

½   cup finely grated Parmesan cheese

2   large eggs

5   tablespoons extra-virgin olive oil, plus more for greasing

Kosher salt and freshly ground black pepper

¾   cup plus 2 tablespoons all-purpose flour

2   tablespoons unsalted butter

2   garlic cloves, thinly sliced

1   (10-ounce) bunch leaf spinach, stemmed, or 5 ounces baby spinach

1   tablespoon fresh lemon juice

Pistachio-Almond Dukka (page 280) or store-bought dukka, for sprinkling

In a food processor, combine the ricotta, Parmesan, eggs, 2 tablespoons of the olive oil, 2 teaspoons salt, and 1 teaspoon pepper and puree until smooth. Scrape down the sides of the bowl and puree again. Add the flour and pulse until the flour is just incorporated. Scrape the gnudi dough into a medium bowl.

Fill a large pot with water and bring to a simmer over medium heat (it should be bubbling but not rapidly boiling) and then add a small handful of salt. Using a 1½-tablespoon ice cream scoop, scoop half the gnudi dough directly into the simmering water. Simmer the gnudi until they rise to the surface, 1 to 2 minutes. Continue

RECIPE CONTINUES

to simmer until the gnudi are cooked through, 5 to 7 minutes more. They should be pillowy but just firm (sacrifice 1 gnudi by cutting it in half to check the doneness). Using a slotted spoon, transfer the gnudi to a lightly oiled baking sheet. Repeat with the remaining gnudi dough. Let stand at room temperature for 10 minutes.

In a large nonstick skillet, melt the butter in 2 tablespoons of the olive oil over medium-high heat. Add the gnudi and cook until browned on the bottom, 3 to 5 minutes. Give the pan a shake and cook until the gnudi are coated in the butter mixture, about 1 minute more. Using a slotted spoon, return the gnudi to the baking sheet.

In the same skillet over medium heat, heat the remaining 1 tablespoon olive oil. Add the garlic and cook, stirring, until softened, about 2 minutes. Add the spinach and a generous pinch of salt and cook, stirring, until just wilted, about 3 minutes. Add the gnudi and 1 tablespoon fresh lemon juice and stir gently to mix.

Season the gnudi and spinach with salt and pepper, then transfer to plates or a platter. Sprinkle with some Pistachio-Almond Dukka and serve.

DO IT AHEAD The cooked gnudi can be refrigerated in an airtight container overnight. Reheat them in simmering water for about 1 minute and then let stand for 10 minutes before browning them in the skillet.

RICE & PORK
CONGEE

with Chiles, Crispy Garlic & Ginger

HANDS-ON TIME
30 MIN

TOTAL TIME
55 MIN

SERVES 4

Steamed rice is one of the most basic foods to make, isn't it? Well, if you've ever gotten distracted while making dinner, you know this statement is bogus. Even with a rice cooker you might end up with mushy, sticky grains. But with the Asian rice porridge called congee, you actually *want* to cook the rice until it's so soft, it suspends itself in its thickened cooking liquid. The trick: Use enough liquid.

8½ cups low-sodium chicken broth

1 cup long-grain white rice

¼ cup canola oil

1 (2-inch) piece fresh ginger, peeled and cut into thin matchsticks

3 large garlic cloves, thinly sliced

½ pound ground pork

2 tablespoons low-sodium soy sauce

Kosher salt

Chopped fresh cilantro, for sprinkling

Thinly sliced scallions, for sprinkling

Thinly sliced hot red chiles, for sprinkling

Sambal oelek or other Asian chile paste, for serving

In a large saucepan, combine the broth, rice, and 2 cups water and bring to a boil over high heat. Simmer over medium-low heat, stirring often, until the congee is thickened and resembles porridge, about 45 minutes.

Meanwhile, in a medium skillet, heat the canola oil over medium heat until shimmering. Add the ginger and garlic and cook, stirring, until golden and crisp, about 5 minutes. Using a slotted spoon, transfer the crispy ginger and garlic to a paper towel–lined plate to drain.

Pour off all but 1 tablespoon of the fat from the skillet. Add the pork and cook over medium heat, breaking up the meat with a wooden spoon, until just cooked through, about 7 minutes. Remove from the heat and stir in the soy sauce. Stir the pork into the congee and season with salt.

Ladle the congee into bowls. Sprinkle with cilantro, scallions, hot red chiles, and the crispy garlic and ginger. Serve right away, passing sambal oelek at the table.

DO IT AHEAD The rice and pork congee can be refrigerated in an airtight container for up to 3 days. Reheat gently, adding a little water if it's too thick. The crispy ginger and garlic can be stored in an airtight container at room temperature for up to 3 days.

QUINOA BURGERS

with Avocado Mayo & Pea Shoots

HANDS-ON TIME
45 MIN

TOTAL TIME
1 HR 10 MIN

SERVES 6

I'm not just a fan of big, juicy hamburgers, I'm a superfan—I'm talkin' obsessed-with-Jake-Gyllenhaal-level superfan. So when I want a real burger, I eat one. But I'm also obsessed with this quinoa burger. Not because it mimics the beef kind, but because it's delicious on its own terms—crispy on the outside, tender on the inside. And it's healthy, too.

Kosher salt

1 cup quinoa, rinsed

3 large eggs

½ cup plain dry bread crumbs

¼ cup finely chopped fresh parsley

1 shallot, minced

2 tablespoons cornstarch

1 garlic clove, minced

1 teaspoon freshly ground black pepper

4 tablespoons extra-virgin olive oil

6 English muffins, split and lightly toasted

Avocado Mayo (page 268) or mayonnaise, for serving

Sliced cucumber, for topping

Pea shoots or lettuce, for topping

Bring a medium saucepan of water to a boil, and add a generous pinch of salt. Add the quinoa and boil over medium-high heat until tender, about 10 minutes. Drain well in a fine sieve and then return to the hot saucepan. Cover and let steam for 10 minutes, then fluff with a fork and spread on a large plate to cool.

In a large bowl, combine the quinoa, eggs, bread crumbs, parsley, shallot, cornstarch, garlic, pepper, and 1½ teaspoons salt. Mix well and let stand for 10 minutes. Using a ½-cup measure, scoop packed mounds of the quinoa mixture onto a waxed paper–lined plate. Using a damp hand, gently press them into ¾-inch-thick patties. Refrigerate for 15 minutes.

Preheat the oven to 200°F.

In a large nonstick skillet, heat 2 tablespoons of the olive oil over medium-high heat until shimmering. Add 3 of the quinoa patties and cook until browned and crusty on the bottom, about 3 minutes. Using a spatula, carefully flip the patties and cook until browned and cooked through, about 3 minutes more. Transfer to a baking sheet and put in the oven to keep warm. Repeat with the remaining 2 tablespoons olive oil and 3 patties.

Spread the cut sides of the English muffins with Avocado Mayo. Place the quinoa burgers on the muffin bottoms, top with sliced cucumber and pea shoots, and serve.

DO IT AHEAD The formed quinoa patties can be refrigerated, covered, overnight. Alternatively, freeze the uncooked patties on a baking sheet and when firm, transfer them to a plastic bag and freeze for up to 1 month. Defrost them before cooking.

HEATHER'S
RED RICE

HANDS-ON TIME
15 MIN

TOTAL TIME
45 MIN

SERVES 4 TO 6

For my sixteenth birthday, my sister Heather threw me a small family party at her house. She has a son named Gilbert who, to this day, we all call Pa. He was very young then, and, you know, it wasn't easy for her and her husband. They struggled, like many people, to give him what he needed and wanted while taking care of themselves. So when Heather asked me what I wanted for my birthday, I asked her to teach me how to make her red rice. Better than any rice I'd ever eaten at a restaurant, it was tender and fluffy with the perfect amount of tomato.

The key, she explained during our lesson, was getting the correct rice-to-liquid ratio. But she didn't use a measuring cup. She'd just add water, then stick her index finger right into the skillet, resting the tip on the rice. She knew she had the right amount of water when it reached her first joint. If it was above the crease in her finger she'd scoop some out (always with the empty tomato sauce can), or she'd add a little more water if it didn't quite reach.

My version of her rice offers exact measurements, but I encourage you to test her method. You might just pass the technique down through your family, too.

¼ cup extra-virgin olive oil

1 medium onion, finely chopped

Kosher salt

1½ cups long-grain white rice (I like to use jasmine rice)

1 (8-ounce) can tomato sauce

1 medium tomato, finely diced

Chopped fresh cilantro, for sprinkling

Crumbled queso fresco or farmer cheese (optional), for sprinkling

In a large nonstick skillet, heat the olive oil over medium-high heat until shimmering. Add the onion and a generous pinch of salt and cook, stirring occasionally, until softened and just starting to brown, about 8 minutes. Add the rice and cook, stirring, until the rice is coated and starts to lighten in color around the edges, 2 to 3 minutes.

Stir the tomato sauce, tomato, and 2½ cups water into the rice. Season the cooking liquid generously with salt and bring to a boil over high heat. Stir the rice once, cover, and simmer over low heat until the rice is tender and all the water has been absorbed, about 20 minutes. Remove from the heat and let steam for 10 minutes, then fluff with a fork.

Sprinkle with chopped cilantro and crumbled queso fresco, if desired, and serve.

DO IT AHEAD The red rice can be refrigerated in an airtight container overnight. Cover with a damp paper towel and reheat gently in the microwave before serving.

STOVETOP
MAC 'N' CHEESE
with Bacon Bread Crumbs

HANDS-ON TIME
25 MIN

TOTAL TIME
35 MIN

SERVES 4 TO 6

I grew up eating boxed macaroni and cheese. It was one of the first things I was allowed to make on my own, other than ketchup sandwiches, and that made me proud. Recently I decided I'd try it again because, you know, there's a definite place and time for boxed macaroni and cheese. No judgments. It tasted exactly as I remembered, but I certainly didn't love it the way I thought I would. To make myself feel better, I created this version, packed with sharp white cheddar. You can skip the crispy bacon crumbs, if you like (even though I could eat them by the handful), and sprinkle some chopped toasted hazelnuts on top for an elegant twist. Or, heck, throw on some crispy onions from a can.

Kosher salt

4 bacon slices, finely chopped

½ cup panko bread crumbs

Freshly ground black pepper

1 pound medium pasta shells

4 tablespoons (½ stick) unsalted butter

3 tablespoons all-purpose flour

3½ cups whole milk

8 ounces extra-sharp white cheddar cheese, shredded

1 tablespoon Dijon mustard

Chopped fresh chives, for sprinkling

Bring a large saucepan of water to a boil, and add a small handful of salt.

In a medium skillet, cook the bacon over medium-high heat, stirring, until rendered and lightly browned but not crisp, 3 to 5 minutes. Add the panko and cook, stirring, until the bacon is crisp and the panko is golden, about 3 minutes. Remove from the heat and season the bacon bread crumbs with salt and pepper.

Cook the pasta shells in the boiling water according to the package directions until al dente, 8 to 10 minutes. Drain well in a colander. Add 1 tablespoon of the butter to the hot noodles and toss well to prevent sticking.

In the same large saucepan, melt the remaining 3 tablespoons butter over medium-high heat. Add the flour and cook, whisking continuously, until a bubbling paste forms, about 2 minutes. Gradually whisk in the milk and bring to a boil. Simmer over medium heat, whisking, until thickened and no floury taste remains, about 7 minutes. Whisk in the cheese, mustard, and 2 teaspoons pepper until the sauce is smooth. Stir in the pasta shells and season with salt.

Serve hot, sprinkled with the bacon bread crumbs and chopped chives.

QUINOA-PORK
LARB

HANDS-ON TIME
35 MIN

TOTAL TIME
55 MIN

SERVES 6

At home, Jason always wants meat or fish for dinner, while I could easily be satisfied with a big ol' bowl of grains. This recipe is our happy compromise. Larb, a type of warm salad often eaten in Laos and northern Thailand, is traditionally made with a range of proteins from raw beef to duck. I use half pork and half quinoa, perk it up with fresh herbs, lime juice, Sriracha, and fish sauce, and serve it in lettuce cups.

Kosher salt

1 cup quinoa, rinsed

1 tablespoon canola oil

½ pound ground pork

Freshly ground black pepper

⅓ cup fresh lime juice, plus wedges for serving

2 tablespoons Asian fish sauce

2 tablespoons minced shallot

1½ teaspoons sriracha, plus more for serving

1 teaspoon light brown sugar

1 garlic clove, finely grated

1 cup chopped fresh cilantro, plus more for serving

1 cup chopped fresh mint, plus more for serving

Lettuce leaves, such as Bibb or iceberg, for serving

Bring a medium saucepan of water to a boil, and add a generous pinch of salt. Add the quinoa and boil over medium-high heat until tender, about 10 minutes. Drain well in a fine sieve and then return to the hot saucepan. Cover and let steam for 10 minutes, then fluff with a fork.

Meanwhile, in a large skillet, heat the canola oil over medium-high heat. Add the pork and cook, breaking up the meat with a wooden spoon, until just cooked through, about 7 minutes. Season the pork with salt and pepper.

In a large bowl, whisk together the lime juice, fish sauce, shallot, sriracha, brown sugar, and garlic. Add the quinoa and pork and mix well. Fold in the cilantro and mint and season the larb with salt and pepper.

Serve the quinoa-pork larb in lettuce cups, passing lime wedges, sriracha, cilantro, and mint at the table.

DO IT AHEAD The cooked quinoa can be refrigerated in an airtight container for up to 3 days. Warm gently in the microwave before mixing with the other ingredients.

SEAFOOD

I CAN'T BELIEVE HOW MANY PEOPLE think seafood is the most intimidating thing to cook. Actually, it's exactly the opposite. If you really think about it, some of the best seafood recipes require almost no prep. Salmon sashimi, oysters on the half shell, and tuna tartare are practically ready to eat right out of the ocean! Even baked sole is fantastic with just a sprinkle of salt and a squeeze of lemon. I've been on a mission lately to get my friends and family to cook more fish at home. Whether you bake, steam, or fry your seafood, don't let it stress you out. Just cook it!

CATALAN-STYLE
MUSSELS
with Green Olives
& Fried Almonds
184

GREEN
CURRY
with Halibut & Basil
185

CRISPY FISH STICK
TACOS
with Herb Salad
186

Baked
FISH
with Lime Sauce
188

Marinated
TUNA
with Peppers & Olives
189

Peel-&-Eat
SHRIMP
with Green Chile Butter
191

Potato-Crusted
TROUT SCHNITZEL
with Caper Mayo
192

BUTTER-BASTED
SCALLOPS
with Watercress & Charred Corn
193

LESSON:
EN PAPILLOTE,
A LOVE LETTER
196

SEA BASS
& BABY BOK CHOY
in Parchment
198

SALMON
with Haricots Verts
& Tomatoes
in Parchment
199

HALIBUT,
Sweet Corn & Mushrooms
in Parchment
202

CATALAN-STYLE
MUSSELS

with Green Olives & Fried Almonds

HANDS-ON TIME
25 MIN

TOTAL TIME
30 MIN

SERVES 4

When it comes to mussels, I'm much more interested in an intensely delicious cooking broth than I am in the mollusks themselves. But Jason is a mussels maniac. So I created this recipe to please both of us. The fried almonds not only add a ton of flavor, they also let me sprinkle on a little crunch.

1 pound ripe tomatoes, halved crosswise

⅓ cup extra-virgin olive oil

½ cup whole raw almonds

1 medium red onion, finely chopped

3 large garlic cloves, thinly sliced

1 cup green olives, pitted and chopped

½ cup dry white wine

2 tablespoons unsalted butter

½ teaspoon red pepper flakes

4 pounds small to medium mussels, scrubbed and debearded

Chopped fresh parsley, for sprinkling

Crusty bread, for serving

Working over a bowl, grate the cut side of the tomato halves on the large holes of a box grater until only the skin remains in your hand; discard the skins.

In a large pot, heat the olive oil over medium-high heat. Add the almonds and cook, stirring, until golden and fragrant, 3 to 5 minutes. Using a slotted spoon, transfer to a paper towel–lined plate to drain, then finely chop.

Add the onion and garlic to the pot and cook over medium-high heat, stirring occasionally, until the onion is just softened, 3 to 5 minutes. Add the grated tomatoes, olives, wine, butter, and red pepper flakes and bring to a boil. Stir in the mussels, cover, and cook over high heat, shaking the pan a couple of times, until the mussels open, about 5 minutes. Transfer the mussels to a large serving platter and pour everything from the pot on top. Sprinkle with parsley and the chopped fried almonds. Serve with crusty bread.

TIP Cleaning mussels is easier than you think. Invert a small plate into the bottom of a big bowl (one that'll fit in your fridge) and put the mussels on top, then fill the bowl with water. Add a huge pinch—I'm talking a 5-finger pinch—each of kosher salt and fine cornmeal, and then refrigerate them for 30 minutes. The salt and cornmeal encourage the mussels to spit out excess debris and the plate allows the debris to fall beneath the mussels. After 30 minutes, use a paring knife to scrape off any barnacles and to help pull out the beard.

GREEN CURRY

with Halibut & Basil

TOTAL TIME
30 MIN

SERVES 4

I use green curry paste all the time (check out my recipe for Thai beef salad on page 120) because it's so packed with flavor that it can replace a slew of other ingredients. Here it becomes the base for a sauce that is truly versatile, delicious with whatever you have on hand. I use halibut because it holds up well in a quick braise, but swordfish is even better if you don't mind paying a little extra. Jason loves this recipe because he can never get enough fish—especially halibut—and because he's into any dish that comes with a sauce he can sop up with rice.

2   ears corn, husks and silks removed

3   tablespoons canola oil

¼   cup Thai green curry paste

½   cup unsweetened coconut milk

1   (8-ounce) bottle clam juice

1   red bell pepper, cut into 1-inch pieces

1   pound skinless halibut fillet, cut into 1-inch cubes

4   ounces sugar snap peas, strings removed

2   tablespoons fresh lime juice, plus wedges for serving

Kosher salt and freshly ground black pepper

Small or torn fresh basil leaves, for topping

Very thinly sliced jalapeño, for topping

Steamed rice, for serving

Invert a small bowl and place it in the bottom of a large bowl. Working with one ear at a time, stand the corn on the small bowl and, using a knife, cut off the kernels so that they fall into the large bowl. Remove the small bowl. You should have about 1 cup fresh kernels.

In a large deep skillet, heat the canola oil over medium-high heat. Add the curry paste and cook, stirring, until sizzling and fragrant, about 3 minutes. Whisk in the coconut milk and clam juice and bring to a simmer. Add the bell pepper and corn kernels and simmer, stirring occasionally, until the vegetables are softened slightly but still crisp, about 5 minutes. Add the halibut and snap peas and simmer over medium heat, stirring gently, until the fish is just cooked through (it should be white throughout) and the snap peas are crisp-tender, about 5 minutes. Stir in the lime juice and season with salt and black pepper.

Ladle the curry into bowls and top with the basil and jalapeño. Serve hot, with steamed rice.

CRISPY FISH STICK TACOS

with Herb Salad

TOTAL TIME
30 MIN

SERVES 4

As a kid, I was infatuated with frozen fish sticks (Gorton's, I think the brand was), which I stuffed into tortillas along with lettuce and hot sauce. My tastes have changed since then but my love for fish sticks has not. Nor has my preferred way of eating them. This is my modern version, the biggest fish stick upgrade of all time.

1   cup all-purpose flour

3   large eggs

    Kosher salt

2   cups panko bread crumbs

    Freshly ground black pepper

    Two 8-ounce skinless swordfish steaks (½ inch thick), cut into ½-inch-wide sticks

1½ tablespoons canola or vegetable oil, plus more for frying

1½ cups lightly packed fresh cilantro leaves

¾   cup snipped fresh chives

¾   cup snipped fresh dill

1   Fresno chile or jalapeño, halved, and very thinly sliced

2½ tablespoons fresh lime juice

    Sour cream, for spreading

12 corn tortillas, warmed

    Lime wedges, for serving

Spread the flour in a shallow bowl. In another shallow bowl, beat the eggs with a pinch of salt. Spread the panko in another bowl and season with salt and pepper.

Season the swordfish sticks with salt and pepper. In batches, dredge the sticks in the flour. Dip the sticks in the egg, allowing the excess to drip off, then dredge in the panko. Transfer to a plate.

In a large skillet, heat ¼ inch of canola oil over medium-high heat until shimmering (the oil is ready if you stick the end of a wooden spoon in the center and bubbles form around it). Add the coated fish sticks and fry, turning once, until browned and cooked through, about 5 minutes total. Transfer to paper towels to drain and season lightly with salt.

Meanwhile, in a medium bowl, toss the cilantro, chives, dill, chile, lime juice, and canola oil. Season the herb salad with salt and pepper. Spread sour cream on the warm tortillas and top with the fish sticks and herb salad. Serve with lime wedges.

BAKED FISH

with Lime Sauce

HANDS-ON TIME
15 MIN

TOTAL TIME
30 MIN

SERVES 4

Baked fish doesn't sound so glamorous but I promise you that once you try this incredibly easy recipe, you'll want to bake *all* your fish. First off, this method keeps the fish moist and tender. Then there's the smell factor. Unless you have a superior vent hood over your stove (sigh, I don't), then baking's the way to go. Still not convinced? Give this recipe a try. The tangy, herbal, savory sauce is to die for.

2 tablespoons canola or vegetable oil

4 (6-ounce) skinless sea bass fillets, about 1 inch thick

Kosher salt and freshly ground black pepper

¼ cup fresh lime juice

2 tablespoons Asian fish sauce

2 tablespoons minced fresh cilantro

1 small serrano chile, seeded and minced

1 teaspoon sugar

Steamed rice, for serving

Preheat the oven to 425°F.

Pour the canola oil over the bottom of a large ceramic or glass baking dish. Add the fish fillets and turn to coat in the oil. Season the fish all over with salt and pepper. Bake for 12 to 15 minutes, until the fish is just cooked through (you should be able to flake it with a fork—but don't flake too much, be gentle).

Meanwhile, in a small bowl, whisk together the lime juice, fish sauce, cilantro, chile, and sugar.

Transfer the fish to plates and serve with the lime sauce and steamed rice.

MARINATED TUNA

with Peppers & Olives

HANDS-ON TIME
15 MIN

TOTAL TIME
1 HR 15 MIN

SERVES 4

When I was in grade school, my grandma would sometimes pack me lunches of tuna salad and sliced cucumbers. I used to get embarrassed to eat them in front of my friends because they'd all have Lunchables and other exotica.

Nowadays, tuna with peppers and olives is my ideal lunch. This recipe is packed with different flavors and textures, plus a marinade (aka dressing) that I can sop up with a little bread. This ritual slows me down as I eat and reminds me to appreciate what I have.

½ cup red wine vinegar

½ cup extra-virgin olive oil

2 tablespoons minced shallot

1 tablespoon fresh thyme leaves

Kosher salt and freshly ground black pepper

2 (5-ounce) cans good-quality solid white tuna in olive oil, drained and broken into large chunks

¾ cup pitted Castelvetrano olives, lightly crushed

½ cup piquillo peppers, quartered and seeded

½ cup sweet or spicy Peppadew peppers, halved

Warm crusty bread or crackers, for serving

In a small bowl, whisk together the vinegar, olive oil, shallot, and thyme. Season the marinade generously with salt and black pepper.

Scatter the tuna, olives, and both peppers evenly over the bottom of a small baking dish or large shallow bowl. Whisk the marinade again, then pour it evenly over the tuna, olives, and peppers. Cover with plastic wrap and marinate in the refrigerator overnight.

Return the marinated tuna to room temperature. Using a slotted spoon, transfer to plates. Spoon some of the marinade on top and serve with crusty bread or crackers.

DO IT AHEAD The marinated tuna can be refrigerated in an airtight container for up to 3 days.

PEEL-&-EAT
SHRIMP

with Green Chile Butter

HANDS-ON TIME
15 MIN

TOTAL TIME
30 MIN

SERVES 4 TO 6

I have some issues with shrimp. I find them just too easy to overcook, seizing up and becoming chewy and tough. I prefer my shrimp to be juicy and tender, with no chewy brown bits. All this explains why I have a thing for peel-and-eat shrimp. They might be a little messy to eat, but cooking them in the shell helps protect their delicate texture. I split the shrimp along the back to remove the veins and spread them with a green chile butter before roasting them in the oven. They're done when they're steamy and just white throughout.

6 tablespoons (¾ stick) unsalted butter, at room temperature or softened in the microwave

2 medium jalapeños or serrano chiles, seeded and minced

2 tablespoons minced fresh chives

1 teaspoon finely grated lemon zest

Kosher salt and freshly ground black pepper

1½ pounds shell-on extra-large shrimp

Lemon wedges, for serving

Preheat the oven to 475°F.

In a small bowl, using a fork, blend the butter, jalapeños, chives, lemon zest, and a generous pinch each of salt and pepper.

Using the tip of a pair of scissors, cut along the back of the shrimp through the shell, leaving the shell intact. Using a small knife, remove and discard the vein. Using a small spoon or table knife, spread the green chile butter on the exposed shrimp and under the shell. Refrigerate for 15 minutes.

Spread the shrimp in an even layer on a large rimmed baking sheet and season with salt and pepper. Roast for 10 to 12 minutes, until the shrimp are just cooked through; flip the shrimp halfway through cooking. Let cool slightly, then serve with lemon wedges.

DO IT AHEAD   The green chile butter can be refrigerated in an airtight container for up to 3 days. Bring to room temperature before using.

POTATO-CRUSTED TROUT SCHNITZEL

with Caper Mayo

TOTAL TIME
30 MIN

SERVES 4

Instant mashed potatoes are one of my niftiest cooking hacks. Every now and then I'll catch Jason whisking some in butter and hot milk to make a secret snack. But my MO is to use the flakes as a gluten-free substitute for bread crumbs or flour, whether for thickening soups or coating chicken, fish, or pork to make schnitzel. Try it with the trout here and you'll be proudly stocking up on instant mashed potatoes, too.

¼ cup mayonnaise

2 tablespoons minced fresh chives

1½ tablespoons drained capers, finely chopped

2 teaspoons fresh lemon juice

Kosher salt and freshly ground black pepper

2 large eggs

1½ cups dried potato flakes (aka instant mashed potatoes)

4 (6-ounce) skin-on trout fillets, pin bones removed (see Tip)

½ cup extra-virgin olive oil

Mixed greens salad, for serving

In a small bowl, whisk together the mayonnaise, chives, capers, and lemon juice. Season the caper mayo with salt and pepper.

In a shallow bowl or pie plate, beat the eggs with a pinch each of salt and pepper. Spread the potato flakes in another shallow bowl. Using a paring knife, make four or five very shallow slits in the skin of the trout (this will help prevent it from curling in the pan). Season the fillets with salt and pepper. Dip the fillets in the egg, letting the excess drip back in the bowl. Dredge them in the potato flakes, pressing lightly to help the flakes adhere, and transfer to a plate.

In a large nonstick skillet, heat the olive oil over medium-high heat until shimmering. Add the trout fillets skin-side down and cook until browned and crisp on the bottom, 3 to 4 minutes. Using a thin spatula, carefully flip the fillets and cook until the other side is browned and the fish is cooked through, about 3 minutes more. Transfer the fish to paper towels to drain, then transfer to plates and serve with the caper mayo and a mixed greens salad.

TIP Your first step to ensuring your fillets do not have pin bones is to ask your fishmonger to remove them. If you happen to get the fillets home only to find some pin bones remaining, I've got a brilliant trick for removing them. You need two tools: a medium bowl and needle-nose pliers (the ones you keep devoted to food!). Invert the bowl on a work surface. Lay the fish skin-side down over the inverted bowl. The edges of the bowl will pull the fillet taut while also pushing out the pin bones just enough that you can snag them easily with the pliers.

BUTTER-BASTED
SCALLOPS
with Watercress & Charred Corn

TOTAL TIME
30 MIN

SERVES 4

The key to perfect scallops is quite simple really: Don't overcook them! Heck, I love to eat them raw and have friends who really only ever eat them that way (paging Kate Heddings and Kay Chun). If you're not into that, try my trick: Cook them longer on one side, then finish them for just a minute or two on the other. That way you'll end up with scallops that are just cooked all the way through, so they're opaque and not entirely firm, or slightly underdone.

1   small red onion, halved and very thinly sliced

4   ears corn, husks and silks removed

3   tablespoons extra-virgin olive oil, plus more for rubbing

    Kosher salt and freshly ground black pepper

1   (6-ounce) bunch watercress, thick stems discarded

2   tablespoons apple cider vinegar

16 large sea scallops (1½ pounds)

2   tablespoons unsalted butter

    Lemon wedges, for serving

Fill a medium bowl with ice and water. Add the red onion and refrigerate until chilled and crisp, about 15 minutes. Drain the onion and pick out the ice cubes, then spread the onion on paper towels to dry.

Meanwhile, light a grill or preheat a grill pan over medium-high heat. Rub the corn with olive oil and season with salt and pepper. Grill, turning occasionally, until lightly charred and the kernels are crisp-tender, about 10 minutes. Transfer to a work surface and let cool slightly.

Invert a small bowl and place it in the bottom of a large bowl. Working with one ear at a time, stand the corn on the small bowl and, using a knife, cut off the kernels so they fall into the large bowl. Remove the small bowl. You should have about 2 cups fresh kernels. Add the watercress, vinegar, drained red onion, and 2 tablespoons of the olive oil. Season with salt and pepper and toss well. Transfer the salad to individual plates or a serving platter.

Season the scallops generously with salt and pepper. In a large nonstick skillet, heat the remaining 1 tablespoon olive oil over high heat. Add the scallops and cook until browned and crisp on the bottom, about 3 minutes. Working quickly, flip the scallops and add the butter to the skillet. Cook, spooning the butter over the scallops, until they are barely firm to the touch, 1 to 2 minutes more. Spoon the scallops and butter over the salad, garnish with lemon wedges, and serve right away.

Butter-Basted
SCALLOPS
*with Watercress
& Charred Corn*
PAGE 193

LESSON: EN PAPILLOTE, A LOVE LETTER

If there's one thing I've learned from cooking in a tiny New York City apartment without great venting, it's that cooking *en papillote* is by far the best method for making seafood. Cooking *en papillote*—in parchment—allows you to essentially steam fish with aromatics and vegetables in their own flavorful juices along with whatever other liquids you choose to use. It's often thought of as a fussy "diet food" technique when it's actually a very basic method that yields delicious food and just *happens* to be healthy. Plus, once it's done, you're literally tossing the cooking vessel in the trash, so cleanup is simple. Here, a few guidelines.

PICK YOUR WRAPPER

Parchment paper is coated to prevent sticking, which is ideal for delicate fish fillets. In a pinch, aluminum foil works well, too. You should use a larger-than-you-think sheet of parchment (I prefer ones that are 15 inches in length for an individual packet) because once you start layering your ingredients, it's easier to cut off any excess than to transfer everything to a new sheet if it's not big enough. Plus, you want enough paper to fold over the ingredients so that there's just enough room for the steam to rise.

CHOOSE YOUR INGREDIENTS

Less is more when cooking *en papillote*: The more you squeeze into your parcel, the harder it is to wrap up. Start by choosing your fish and then pair it with ingredients that complement its flavor. If you choose a fattier fish, like salmon, choose more acidic ingredients (tomatoes, citrus) for balance. Likewise, lean fish, like sea bass, pairs well with ingredients that get juicy when steamed, like zucchini and mushrooms.

HARNESS THE POWER OF HERBS

Jack up the flavor of your parcels with herbs sprigs, like basil and cilantro. You can easily pick them out at the end when they're wilted. Alternatively, sprinkle on chopped fresh herbs.

MAKE AN INSTANT SAUCE

Here's where things get fun! Drizzle on a little wine, soy sauce, or citrus juice. Butter, cream, and nut oils—sesame, walnut, pistachio—lend a luscious quality that's especially important when using lean fish.

SEAL THE DEAL

Parchment can be a little tricky to use at first, but you'll get the hang of it. Just arrange sheets on a work surface and pile ingredients on one half. Fold the parchment over the ingredients and then, starting at one end, fold over the edge and crimp to seal. Continue folding over and crimping the edge at 1-inch intervals until you reach the opposite end, then twist the corner to make it airtight.

HIT THE (BAKING) SHEETS

Always bake your parcels on a large rimmed baking sheet. It's easier to move them about and you prevent any totally avoidable mishaps. Once you get them in a hot oven (I'm talking 425°F), leave them alone for usually around 10 to 15 minutes until they're super puffy, which generally is your sign that the ingredients are cooked. Snip open the packets with scissors (be careful of the steam) and serve in the parchment, or just slide everything onto a plate.

THINK BIG

Typically when cooking *en papillote*, it's more common to make individual packets—they're easier to move around and serve. But because I'm the adventurous type, I often make one outrageously oversized packet packed with enough ingredients to serve four. For this method, I use a 3-foot-long sheet of parchment and up the cooking time by about 5 minutes.

SEA BASS
& BABY BOK CHOY
in Parchment

HANDS-ON TIME
20 MIN

TOTAL TIME
40 MIN

SERVES 4

I should call this recipe "Jason's Favorite Sea Bass" because he asks me to make it just about every other day. I happen to think it's the ideal recipe because the bok choy and the fish steam in the same amount of time, creating a delectable broth. And did I mention it's healthy?

4   (5- to 6-ounce) skin-on black sea bass fillets, rinsed and patted dry

Kosher salt and freshly ground black pepper

4   (4- to 5-ounce) heads baby bok choy, halved lengthwise and cut crosswise into 2-inch pieces

¼   cup dry white wine

8   teaspoons low-sodium soy sauce

4   teaspoons peeled and minced fresh ginger

1   teaspoon toasted sesame oil

Steamed rice, for serving

Preheat the oven to 425°F.

Season both sides of the sea bass fillets with salt and pepper.

Lay four 15-inch-long sheets of parchment paper on a work surface. Divide the baby bok choy among the sheets and season lightly with salt and pepper. Top each mound with a sea bass fillet, 1 tablespoon of the wine, 2 teaspoons of the soy sauce, 1 teaspoon of the ginger, and ¼ teaspoon of the sesame oil. Season lightly with salt and pepper.

Form one packet at a time: Fold the parchment over the fish and then, starting at one end, fold over the edge and crimp it to seal. Continue folding over and crimping the edge at 1-inch intervals until you reach the opposite end, then twist the corner to make it airtight.

Transfer the packets to a large rimmed baking sheet. Bake for about 12 minutes, until the parchment is puffed and browned. Transfer the packets to plates and, using scissors, snip open the packet to release the steam (be careful—it's hot). Serve right away with steamed rice.

SALMON with HARICOTS VERTS & TOMATOES

in Parchment

HANDS-ON TIME
20 MIN

TOTAL TIME
40 MIN

SERVES 4

Most people want their salmon with a crisp golden crust. Not me. One of my favorite ways to cook salmon is poaching, and the *en papillote* method yields a very similar result—tender and juicy and not at all oily, like salmon can sometimes be. The cherry tomatoes in the bundle make the fish even better, adding a little tartness to cut the richness.

4 (5- to 6-ounce) salmon fillets (skinless or not, up to you), rinsed and patted dry

Kosher salt and freshly ground black pepper

½ pound haricots verts, stem ends trimmed

1 pint grape or cherry tomatoes, halved if large

2 garlic cloves, minced

1 lemon, thinly sliced and seeded

2 tablespoons extra-virgin olive oil

Crusty bread, for serving

Preheat the oven to 425°F.

Season both sides of the salmon fillets with salt and pepper.

Lay a 3-foot-long piece of parchment paper on a large rimmed baking sheet. Mound the haricot verts, tomatoes, and garlic on one half of the parchment paper and season with salt and pepper. Arrange the salmon fillets and lemon slices on top. Drizzle with the olive oil. Fold the parchment over the fish and then, starting at one end, fold over the edge and crimp it to seal. Continue folding over and crimping the edge at 1-inch intervals until you reach the opposite end, then twist the corner to make it airtight. Bake the packet for 15 minutes for medium salmon and 20 minutes for well-done.

Using scissors, snip open the packet to release the steam (be careful—it's hot). Using a spoon, transfer the salmon, vegetables, and any juices to a deep platter or four shallow bowls. Serve right away with crusty bread.

RECIPE CONTINUES

Mound the ingredients on the parchment and drizzle with olive oil.

Fold the parchment over the ingredients.

SALMON

with Haricots Verts & Tomatoes

PREP

Fold over the edge and crimp to seal.

Use your finger to crimp the edge at 1-inch intervals.

Continue to fold and crimp all the way around.

Bake the packet for 15 to 20 minutes.

HALIBUT,
SWEET CORN & MUSHROOMS
in Parchment

HANDS-ON TIME
25 MIN

TOTAL TIME
45 MIN

SERVES 4

This recipe is super summery because of the corn but still earthy and hearty because of the mushrooms. If you have time, and I'm not saying this is required, try quick-brining the halibut first. It adds even more flavor and helps season the fish all the way through. Just mix 4 cups water with 1 tablespoon kosher salt and 2 teaspoons sugar, add the fillets, and refrigerate for 30 minutes. Drain the fish and pat dry before cooking.

4   ears corn, husks and silks removed

¾   pound mixed mushrooms, such as cremini and stemmed shiitakes, halved or quartered if large

8   small spring onions, greens cut into 1-inch lengths and bulbs quartered (see Note)

1   lemon, thinly sliced and seeded

    Kosher salt and freshly ground black pepper

4   (5- to 6-ounce) skinless halibut fillets, about 1 inch thick, rinsed and patted dry

2   tablespoons extra-virgin olive oil

2   tablespoons champagne vinegar

2   tablespoons unsalted butter, cut into cubes

1   cup lightly packed torn fresh basil

1   jalapeño, very thinly sliced

Preheat the oven to 425°F.

Invert a small bowl and place it in the bottom of a large bowl. Working with one ear at a time, stand the corn on the small bowl and, using a knife, cut off the kernels so that they fall into the large bowl. Remove the small bowl. You should have about 2 cups fresh kernels. (Feel free to use thawed frozen corn, too, if it's easier.) Add the mushrooms, spring onions, sliced lemon, and a generous pinch each of salt and pepper. Toss to mix the vegetables.

Season the fish on both sides with salt and pepper. Lay a 3-foot-long piece of parchment paper on a large rimmed baking sheet. Mound half the corn-and-mushroom mixture on one half of the parchment paper and top with the halibut fillets. Mound the remaining corn-and-mushroom mixture on the fish. Drizzle the olive oil and vinegar on top and then scatter the butter over everything. Fold the parchment over the fish and then, starting at one end, fold over the edge and crimp it to seal. Continue folding over and crimping the edge at 1-inch intervals until you reach the opposite end, then twist the corner to make it airtight. Bake the packet for 20 minutes, until slightly puffed.

Using scissors, snip open the packet to release the steam (be careful—it's hot). Using a spoon, transfer the vegetables, halibut, and any juices to a deep platter or four shallow bowls. Scatter the basil and jalapeño evenly on top and serve hot.

NOTE If you can't find spring onions, have no fear! You can still make this fantastic recipe. Substitute 8 scallions that have large bulbs on the bottom. If using scallions, there's no need to quarter the bulbs.

MEAT & POULTRY

IF YOU HAVEN'T ALREADY FIGURED IT OUT, I have a passion for all things vegetable. But every now and then I crave a big ol' pot of meatballs or a perfect roast chicken. I just need to decide whether to put all my effort into a recipe that can stand on its own or one that calls out for a fabulous side. I can easily spend all afternoon mulling over this dilemma (welcome to my life!) so I'm filling this chapter with both kinds of dishes. You'll find one-pot meals, including some of the easiest pork carnitas you'll ever make, and recipes that beg for a little side action, like my chicken schnitzel with tangy hot sauce butter.

Roasted
CHICKEN LEGS
with Sourdough Bread
& Poblanos

207

FREE-FORM
CHICKEN
ENCHILADA
STACKS

208

COQ AU VIN
BLANC

211

Flat-Roasted
CHICKENS
with Coriander & Lemon

212

Chicken
SCHNITZEL
with Hot Sauce Butter & Baby
Lettuces

214

SLASHED-&-SUGARED
CHICKEN
DRUMSTICKS

215

OVEN-FRIED
CORNFLAKE
CHICKEN

216

Apple Cider
PULLED CHICKEN
SANDWICHES
with Slaw

220

STEWED BEANS &
SAUSAGE
with Broccoli Rabe

221

Oven-Fried
PORK CARNITAS

223

BLACK PEPPER
PORK
with Asparagus

224

Pork, Scallion & Enoki
NEGIMAKI
with Sesame-Soy Glaze

226

Pineapple-Roasted
PORK SHOULDER

228

GIANT
MEATBALLS
with Marinara Sauce
& Parmesan

229

CLASSIC
MEAT LOAF
SANDWICHES
with Tomato Jam

230

LAMB
ROAST
with Cheater Harissa,
Chickpeas & Kale

232

3-MINUTE
STEAKS
with Carrot Chimichurri

233

THICK
STEAK
with Basil Butter

236

ROASTED CHICKEN LEGS

with Sourdough Bread & Poblanos

HANDS-ON TIME
20 MIN

TOTAL TIME
1 HR 10 MIN

SERVES 4

This is by far my favorite way to roast chicken legs—or any part of the chicken, really—because it creates the ultimate one-pan meal. And if you love croutons as much as I do, you'll appreciate the genius move of roasting the chicken on top of bits of torn sourdough. What happens is the bread absorbs all the rich pan juices and a little bit of fat from the bird, turning addictively chewy on the inside and supremely crispy on the edges—the croutons of your dreams. One quick note about the chiles here: If you can't find poblanos, feel free to substitute cubanelles or another thin-skinned pepper.

½ pound sourdough or other rustic bread, torn into 1½-inch pieces

¼ cup extra-virgin olive oil, plus more for brushing

4 poblano peppers, cut lengthwise into 1-inch strips and seeded

2 red onions, cut through the core into 1-inch wedges

12 garlic cloves, halved

6 fresh oregano sprigs

   Kosher salt and freshly ground black pepper

6 whole chicken legs (2¾ pounds)

2 teaspoons crushed coriander seeds (see Note)

   Lime wedges, for serving

Preheat the oven to 425°F.

On a large rimmed baking sheet, toss the bread with the olive oil, poblanos, onions, garlic, and oregano. Season generously with salt and black pepper. Lightly brush the chicken legs with olive oil and season with salt, black pepper, and the crushed coriander.

Place the chicken on top of the bread and vegetables. Roast for 50 to 55 minutes, until the vegetables are tender and an instant-read thermometer inserted into the thickest chicken thigh registers 160°F. Transfer the chicken, bread, and vegetables to plates and serve with lime wedges.

DO IT AHEAD   Once assembled on the baking sheet, you can refrigerate the uncooked chicken and vegetables for a few hours or overnight. Let stand at room temperature for about 20 minutes before roasting.

NOTE   Crushed coriander seeds lend a fresher flavor than ground coriander; plus, they add fun crunchy texture. To crush them, put the seeds in a small resealable plastic bag and pound them lightly with the bottom of a small skillet.

FREE-FORM CHICKEN ENCHILADA STACKS

HANDS-ON TIME
35 MIN

TOTAL TIME
1 HR

SERVES 4

Enchiladas are corn tortillas rolled around a filling and smothered in sauce. They're soul satisfying, but honestly not so Instagrammable (not that this is ever my sole motivation for making anything, but still). So for a fun variation, I've reimagined the recipe as a tall tortilla tower layered with a simple homemade salsa verde, chicken, and pepper Jack cheese—one of my favorite cheeses for adding lots of flavor fast.

Canola or vegetable oil, for greasing

2 cups finely shredded cooked chicken (from ½ a small rotisserie chicken)

1 (15-ounce) can black beans, drained and rinsed

⅓ cup minced white onion

1 jalapeño, seeded and minced

½ cup finely chopped fresh cilantro, plus leaves for sprinkling

Kosher salt and freshly ground black pepper

12 corn tortillas

3 cups Roasted Salsa Verde (page 39) or store-bought salsa verde

8 ounces pepper Jack cheese, shredded (2 cups)

Hot sauce, for serving

Preheat the oven to 425°F. Line a large rimmed baking sheet with aluminum foil and generously grease it with canola or vegetable oil.

In a large bowl, mix the chicken, beans, onion, jalapeño, and chopped cilantro. Season with salt and pepper and mix again.

Arrange 4 of the tortillas on the prepared baking sheet. Scoop ¼ cup of the Roasted Salsa Verde onto each tortilla. Divide half the chicken mixture evenly on top of the tortillas, then scatter one-third of the cheese evenly on top. Put another tortilla on each stack. Repeat the layering with the salsa verde, chicken mixture, cheese, and tortillas, ending with a final layer of salsa verde and cheese.

Bake the enchilada stacks for about 15 minutes, until the cheese has melted and the tops are lightly browned in spots. Let stand for 10 minutes. Using a large spatula, transfer the stacks to plates and sprinkle with cilantro leaves. Serve with hot sauce.

COQ AU VIN
BLANC

HANDS-ON TIME
40 MIN

TOTAL TIME
1 HR 30 MIN

SERVES 4

When it comes to cooking chicken, there are three essential techniques: roasting, grilling, and, the least appreciated, braising. That brings me to coq au vin, which is one recipe I firmly believe every home cook must conquer. Not because it's a classic but because it teaches you the benefits of braising—ultra-tender meat infused with whatever flavors you choose. This version isn't so traditional (did I hear someone say old-fashioned?) because rather than using red wine, I opt for white. I love the acidity and tang it lends to the chicken and mushrooms.

2 thick-cut bacon slices, chopped

¼ cup extra-virgin olive oil

6 whole chicken legs (2¾ pounds)

Kosher salt and freshly ground black pepper

1 medium onion, finely chopped

1 leek, white and light green parts only, halved lengthwise and cut into 1½-inch lengths

2 medium celery ribs, cut into ¾-inch pieces on an angle

2 garlic cloves, thinly sliced

1½ cups dry white wine

1 cup low-sodium chicken broth

1 pound mixed mushrooms, such as cremini and oyster, cut into 1-inch pieces

Chopped fresh parsley and tarragon, for sprinkling

Crusty bread, for serving

In a large deep skillet, cook the bacon in 2 tablespoons of the olive oil over medium heat, stirring occasionally, until browned but not crisp, about 5 minutes. Using a slotted spoon, transfer the bacon to a plate.

Season the chicken all over with salt and pepper. Add half the chicken to the skillet, skin-side down. Cook over medium heat, turning once, until browned on both sides, 8 to 10 minutes. Transfer to a plate. Repeat with the remaining chicken.

Spoon off all but about 2 tablespoons of fat from the skillet. Add the onion, leek, celery, and garlic and cook over medium heat, stirring occasionally, until just softened, about 5 minutes. Add the wine and broth and bring to a boil over high heat. Stir in the bacon and then nestle the chicken in the sauce. Cover and simmer over low heat until the chicken is very tender, about 45 minutes.

Meanwhile, preheat the oven to 425°F.

On a large rimmed baking sheet, toss the mushrooms with the remaining 2 tablespoons olive oil and season generously with salt and pepper. Roast for about 25 minutes, until tender and lightly browned.

Transfer the chicken to plates or shallow bowls. Stir the mushrooms into the sauce and season with salt and pepper. Spoon the sauce and vegetables around the chicken. Sprinkle with chopped parsley and tarragon and serve with crusty bread.

FLAT-ROASTED CHICKENS

with Coriander & Lemon

HANDS-ON TIME
30 MIN

TOTAL TIME
1 HR 30 MIN

SERVES 6 TO 8

There's nearly nothing better than a perfectly roasted whole chicken. Certainly there are lots of ways to go about it, but I think the most foolproof is cutting out the backbone and cooking the bird flat on a baking sheet, a method called spatchcocking. Why bother? Well, this technique ensures even cooking, so you get a succulent bird every time. Plus, because a spatchcocked chicken is in and out of the oven fast, you can roast it at a much higher temperature—450°F kind of high—without worrying it'll dry out, so you'll get the crispiest skin all over. This recipe lets you roast two birds at once because having extra in the fridge is always a good thing.

2 (3½-pound) whole chickens, patted dry

Extra-virgin olive oil, for rubbing

Kosher salt and freshly ground black pepper

2 tablespoons coriander seeds, crushed (see Note, page 207)

2 tablespoons fresh thyme leaves

1 teaspoon chipotle chile powder or hot paprika

2 lemons

DO IT AHEAD The seasoned uncooked chickens can be refrigerated on the baking sheet, uncovered, overnight. Let stand at room temperature for 30 minutes before roasting.

Preheat the oven to 450°F. Line a large rimmed baking sheet with parchment paper or aluminum foil.

Put one of the chickens breast-side-down on a work surface. Using sturdy kitchen shears, cut along one side of the backbone from the tail end up to the neck. Repeat on the other side to remove the backbone. Using your palms, press firmly on both sides of the chicken to flatten it. Repeat with the other chicken.

Arrange the chickens breast-side down on the prepared baking sheet (it's okay if the ends of the drumsticks hang off a little). Rub them with olive oil and season generously with salt and pepper. Sprinkle the chickens with half the crushed coriander, thyme leaves, and chile powder. Using a fine grater, grate the zest of 1 lemon evenly on top. Flip the chickens over so they're skin-side up. Brush them with olive oil and season generously with salt and pepper. Sprinkle with the remaining coriander, thyme, and chile powder. Grate the zest of the remaining lemon on top. Cut the lemons into quarters and scatter them around the chickens.

Roast the chickens for 50 minutes to 1 hour, until an instant-read thermometer inserted into the thickest part of the breast registers 160°F; rotate the baking sheet halfway through roasting. Transfer the chickens to a carving board and let rest for 10 minutes. Using a large knife, cut the chickens in half by cutting between the breasts, then cut into quarters by cutting between the breast halves and the thighs. Transfer the chicken to plates or a platter and serve with the roasted lemons for squeezing.

CHICKEN SCHNITZEL

with Hot Sauce Butter & Baby Lettuces

HANDS-ON TIME
30 MIN

TOTAL TIME
45 MIN

SERVES 4

If the phrase "hot sauce butter" made you sit up and take notice, you are my kind of cook! Chefs in restaurants have been using flavored butters (aka compound butters) for ages; they're a kitchen ninja's secret weapon for boosting flavor. Here I blend softened butter with Tabasco and parsley, then refrigerate it until just spreadable (sometimes I freeze it to use later). Then I rub it all over pan-fried chicken cutlets right before serving; you could also set it out in a little bowl for dipping, too.

4 tablespoons (½ stick) unsalted butter, melted

2 tablespoons finely chopped fresh parsley

1 tablespoon Tabasco or other Louisiana-style hot sauce

1 large egg

1 tablespoon Dijon mustard

Kosher salt and freshly ground black pepper

1½ cups panko bread crumbs

4 (4-ounce) chicken cutlets (about 2 large breast halves, butterflied and cut in two)

½ cup canola oil

1 (5-ounce) package mixed baby lettuces

1 tablespoon fresh lemon juice

Chopped fresh parsley, for sprinkling

Lemon wedges, for serving

In a small bowl, whisk together the butter, parsley, and hot sauce. Cover and refrigerate the hot sauce butter until spreadable, about 10 minutes.

Meanwhile, in a shallow bowl, beat the egg with the mustard and a generous pinch each of salt and pepper. Spread the panko in another shallow bowl and season lightly with salt and pepper. Season the chicken cutlets with salt and pepper and dip each in the egg mixture, letting the excess drip off. Dredge the chicken cutlets in the panko, pressing to help it adhere. Transfer to a plate.

In a large skillet, heat the canola oil over medium-high heat until shimmering. Add the coated chicken cutlets and cook, turning once, until golden and crisp, about 8 minutes total. Transfer to a paper towel–lined plate to drain briefly, then transfer to individual serving plates.

In a large bowl, toss the baby lettuces with the lemon juice and season with salt and pepper. Pile the salad alongside the chicken schnitzel. Spread some of the butter on the chicken and sprinkle with parsley. Serve with lemon wedges, passing the remaining hot sauce butter at the table.

DO IT AHEAD The hot sauce butter can be refrigerated in an airtight container for up to 5 days.

SLASHED-&-SUGARED

CHICKEN DRUMSTICKS

HANDS-ON TIME
40 MIN

TOTAL TIME
1 HR 10 MIN

SERVES 4 TO 6

I know it sounds a little punk rock, but slashing your chicken is a smart way to let the flavors of the marinade seep all the way in. It also helps the meat cook more quickly on the grill and makes sure you get lots of crispy little caramelized bits. I can't express how much I love it.

12	chicken drumsticks
	Extra-virgin olive oil, for drizzling
	Kosher salt and freshly ground black pepper
1½	tablespoons sugar
1	tablespoon sweet paprika
2	teaspoons ground cumin
	Lime wedges, for serving
	Roasted Salsa Verde (page 39), for serving

Using scissors or a sharp paring knife, slash the drumsticks nearly to the bone in four or five places. Drizzle the drumsticks with olive oil and season generously with salt and pepper. In a small bowl, mix the sugar with the paprika and cumin. Sprinkle the spice-sugar mixture all over the chicken, rubbing it into the slashes. Refrigerate for 30 minutes.

Light a grill and oil the grate. Grill the chicken over medium heat, turning occasionally, until lightly charred and an instant-read thermometer inserted into the thickest drumstick registers 165°F, about 25 minutes. Transfer the chicken to a platter and serve with lime wedges and Roasted Salsa Verde.

TIP If you're not in the mood to grill, or if you don't own one, you can also make these drumsticks in the oven. Roast them on a foil-lined baking sheet in a preheated 425°F degree oven for about 30 minutes, until an instant-read thermometer inserted into the thickest drumstick registers 165°F.

OVEN-FRIED CORNFLAKE CHICKEN

HANDS-ON TIME
15 MIN

TOTAL TIME
1 HR 15 MIN

SERVES 4

I remember the first time Jason made this for me—I couldn't believe he'd choose a recipe that called for *an entire stick of butter*. But I was so impressed by the stupendous crust that I just forced myself to relax. As it happens, a lot of the butter gets left in the baking dish along with the chicken fat that renders during baking. And actually, that's what makes this recipe so genius: The rendered fat and butter come together to fry the chicken right in the oven. I've since adapted the recipe, swapping out the flour coating for crushed cornflakes. I know I'm not the first to use cornflakes this way—I'm probably the trillionth—but I adore what happens when those flakes come together with the nutty flavor of the butter.

6 cups cornflakes

2 large eggs

8 mixed small chicken thighs and drumsticks

Kosher salt and freshly ground black pepper

¾ cup (1½ sticks) unsalted butter

Preheat the oven to 375°F.

Put the cornflakes in a large resealable plastic bag and, using a meat mallet or rolling pin, finely crush them. In a shallow bowl, beat the eggs. Season the chicken generously with salt and pepper. Dip the chicken in the eggs, letting the excess drip back into the bowl, then dredge in the cornflakes and transfer to a plate.

Put the butter in a large ceramic baking dish and put the dish in the oven for about 10 minutes, until the butter has melted. Arrange the chicken in the baking dish, skin-side down. Bake for about 25 minutes, until golden and crisp on the bottom. Flip the chicken and bake for about 25 minutes more, until an instant-read thermometer inserted into the thickest piece registers 165°F. Transfer the chicken to a platter and serve right away.

RECIPE CONTINUES

OVEN-FRIED
CORNFLAKE CHICKEN
PREP

Finely crush the cornflakes in a large resealable plastic bag.

Beat the eggs in a shallow bowl.

Season the chicken with salt and pepper.

Dip the chicken in the eggs.

Add the chicken to the cornflakes.

Shake to coat the chicken in the cornflakes.

Add the coated chicken
to the hot melted
butter, and then fry in
the oven.

APPLE CIDER
PULLED CHICKEN
SANDWICHES

with Slaw

HANDS-ON TIME
30 MIN

TOTAL TIME
6 TO 7 HRS ON
LOW OR 3 TO
4 HRS ON HIGH

SERVES 4

Shockingly, I don't have a BBQ pit behind my New York City apartment. I do own a slow cooker, though, which turns out to be the perfect tool for making succulent pulled-chicken sandwiches. I start out with boneless thighs, because they have so much more flavor than breast meat and hold up better in the slow cooker. In the morning I throw together a sauce—ketchup, apple cider, vinegar—and dump it into the slow cooker with the chicken, then head to work. When I'm back home at the end of the day, I just take two forks to the meat, and dinner is ready. I like to top these sandwiches with my Brussels Sprout, Apple & Pear Slaw, but it's good with any slaw. Remember, the shredded chicken holds up well in the fridge, so don't be afraid to make a little extra.

1   cup apple cider

½   cup ketchup

½   cup packed light brown sugar

¼   cup apple cider vinegar

2   garlic cloves, finely grated

    Kosher salt and freshly ground black pepper

3   pounds boneless, skinless chicken thighs

    Potato buns, split and toasted, for serving

    Brussels Sprout, Apple & Pear Slaw (page 112) or other slaw, for topping

In a slow cooker, whisk together the apple cider, ketchup, sugar, vinegar, garlic, 2 teaspoons salt, and 1 teaspoon pepper. Add the chicken thighs and mix well. Cover and cook on Low for 6 to 7 hours or High for 3 to 4 hours, until the chicken is very tender.

Using two forks, shred the chicken in the sauce and then season generously with salt and pepper.

Pile the pulled chicken on toasted potato buns, top with slaw, and serve.

DO IT AHEAD   The pulled chicken can be refrigerated in an airtight container for up to 3 days. Reheat gently before serving.

STEWED BEANS & SAUSAGE
with Broccoli Rabe

TOTAL TIME
30 MIN

SERVES 4

I'm fixated on the combination of Italian sausage and broccoli rabe. I went through a brief period where I'm pretty sure I ate orecchiette this way at least twice a week. Recently, to switch things up (and make the recipe a little healthier) I've taken a cue from my chef friend Missy Robbins. She sometimes substitutes canned beans for pasta. It's so good, you'll never miss the carbs.

2   tablespoons extra-virgin olive oil

½   pound hot Italian sausage with fennel, casings removed and meat crumbled

1   (15-ounce) can diced tomatoes

Kosher salt and freshly ground black pepper

½   pound broccoli rabe, trimmed and cut into 2-inch pieces

1   (15-ounce) can cannellini beans, drained and rinsed

½   cup low-sodium chicken broth or water

¼   cup chopped fresh parsley

Shaved Parmesan cheese, for sprinkling

Crusty bread, for serving (optional)

In a large deep skillet, heat the olive oil over medium-high heat. Add the sausage and cook, breaking up the meat with a wooden spoon, until the sausage is browned and almost cooked through, about 5 minutes. Add the tomatoes and a generous pinch each of salt and pepper. Simmer, stirring occasionally, until the tomatoes break down, about 5 minutes.

Stir in the broccoli rabe, beans, and broth. Cover partially and simmer over medium heat until the broccoli rabe is wilted and crisp-tender, about 5 minutes. Stir in the parsley and season with salt and pepper.

Sprinkle with shaved Parmesan and serve with crusty bread.

OVEN-FRIED PORK CARNITAS

HANDS-ON TIME
30 MIN

TOTAL TIME
3 HRS 45 MIN

SERVES 6

Traditionally, carnitas are made by combining pork shoulder and assorted aromatics with citrus and some liquids, then braising the whole mess on the stove until the juices evaporate and the pork starts to fry in all the rendered fat. It's a spectacular process, but can also be time-consuming and tedious. My trick for making things simpler: the oven! I braise pork low and slow until tender, then roast it at a higher temperature until the edges become crazy crispy. I like to serve the carnitas in homemade tortillas but store-bought ones keep this recipe easy.

4 pounds pork shoulder, cut into 1½-inch pieces

1 large red onion, cut into 1-inch pieces

15 garlic cloves

1 cup fresh orange juice (from 4 or 5 oranges)

¼ cup extra-virgin olive oil

¼ cup fresh lime juice

1½ tablespoons ancho chile powder or everyday chili powder

1 tablespoon kosher salt

2 teaspoons freshly ground black pepper

To Serve

Warm tortillas

Quick-Pickled Red Onions (page 272)

Diced Hass avocado

Cilantro leaves

Hot sauce

Lime wedges

In a large roasting pan, toss the pork with the onion, garlic, orange juice, olive oil, lime juice, chile powder, salt, and pepper. Marinate at room temperature for 30 minutes.

Preheat the oven to 350°F.

Cover the roasting pan tightly with aluminum foil and roast for about 1 hour 30 minutes, until the pork is very tender.

Increase the oven temperature to 425°F. Uncover the pork and roast for 30 to 40 minutes more, stirring once or twice while roasting, until the pork is crisp on the edges but still juicy and tender (most of the juices should evaporate, that way the pork will fry in its own fat and get all crispy and awesome). Let the pork stand for 15 minutes.

Using two forks, shred the pork. Serve with warm tortillas, Quick-Pickled Red Onions, diced avocado, cilantro leaves, hot sauce, and lime wedges.

DO IT AHEAD The carnitas can be refrigerated in an airtight container for up to 5 days. Reheat in a preheated 350°F oven for about 30 minutes, until hot.

BLACK PEPPER
PORK

with Asparagus

TOTAL TIME
30 MIN
SERVES 4

Here's a recipe that showcases the awesome versatility of pork tenderloin. I halve the meat lengthwise and then thinly slice it crosswise, leaving me with little pieces that cook up quickly in a stir-fry. Please don't forget, pork tenderloin is super lean, so you want to just cook it through. That's why stir-frying is such a good method here—if you're on your game, the meat will be tender, not chewy.

1 (1-pound) pork tenderloin

3 tablespoons low-sodium soy sauce

1 tablespoons cornstarch

1 tablespoon freshly ground black pepper

Kosher salt

3 tablespoons canola or vegetable oil

1 pound asparagus, cut on an angle into 1-inch pieces

Toasted sesame seeds, for sprinkling

Thinly sliced scallions, for sprinkling

Steamed rice, for serving

On a work surface, using a large knife, cut the pork tenderloin in half lengthwise and then cut it crosswise into thin slices. In a large bowl, mix the pork with the soy sauce, cornstarch, pepper, and a generous pinch of salt. Let stand for 15 minutes.

Heat a large cast-iron skillet over high heat. Add 2 tablespoons of the canola oil and swirl to coat the pan. Add the pork and, using a slotted spoon, spread it in an even layer. Cook, undisturbed, until browned on the bottom, 3 to 5 minutes. Continue to cook, stirring, until just cooked through, about 2 minutes more. Transfer to a plate.

Add the remaining 1 tablespoon oil to the hot skillet. Add the asparagus and a generous pinch of salt and cook over medium-high heat, stirring, until the asparagus is crisp-tender, about 3 minutes. Return the pork to the skillet and cook, stirring, until hot, about 1 minute. Season the stir-fry with salt.

Sprinkle with toasted sesame seeds and thinly sliced scallions. Serve hot with steamed rice.

PORK, SCALLION & ENOKI
NEGIMAKI

with Sesame-Soy Glaze

HANDS-ON TIME
50 MIN

TOTAL TIME
1 HR

SERVES 4

Pork tenderloin is way more versatile than most people realize. Cooks tend to roast it whole, but you can do so much more with it; when I'm grilling, for instance, I like to cook chunks of the pork on skewers, or butterfly a roast, rub it with smoked paprika, and throw it on the grate. Here I slice it and lightly pound the slices into thin rounds to wrap around enoki mushrooms and scallions and grill in an umami-rich soy glaze until nicely charred. Just be careful to leave the meat over the heat just until it's cooked through, because pork tenderloin is so lean that it can quickly become chalky and dry—and no amount of glaze is gonna save it.

¼ cup plus 2 tablespoons low-sodium soy sauce

3 tablespoons dry sherry or dry white wine

1½ tablespoons sugar

1 teaspoon toasted sesame seeds, plus more for sprinkling

½ teaspoon toasted sesame oil

1 (1-pound) pork tenderloin

2 bunches scallions

Canola oil, for brushing

Kosher salt and freshly ground black pepper

1 (3½-ounce) bunch enoki mushrooms, roots trimmed and mushrooms separated

Lime wedges, for serving

In a small saucepan, whisk together the soy sauce, sherry, and sugar and bring to a boil over medium-high heat. Simmer over medium heat, whisking often, until the mixture has reduced to a thin glaze, about 5 minutes. Remove from the heat and stir in the sesame seeds and sesame oil.

On a work surface, using a sharp knife, cut off 2 inches from the tapered end of the pork. Cut the rest of the pork crosswise into ½-inch-thick slices. Using a meat mallet or rolling pin, lightly pound all the pork to ⅛ inch thick.

Light a grill or preheat a grill pan over medium heat. Brush the scallions with canola oil and season lightly with salt and pepper. Grill, turning once or twice, until lightly charred, 1 to 2 minutes. Let cool slightly, then cut in half crosswise.

On the work surface, spread out the pounded pork slices and season them lightly with salt and pepper. Divide the scallion halves and enoki mushrooms evenly across the lower edges of the pork slices, then roll them up very tightly.

Lightly brush the pork rolls with canola oil and grill over medium heat, turning occasionally, until lightly charred on the outside and barely cooked through, 8 to 10 minutes. Brush the pork rolls all over with the glaze and grill, turning and brushing, until glazed and just cooked through, 1 to 2 minutes more. Transfer the pork rolls to a clean work surface and cut crosswise into 1-inch lengths.

Transfer the negimaki to a platter and drizzle with any remaining glaze. Sprinkle with toasted sesame seeds and serve with lime wedges.

DO IT AHEAD The glaze can be refrigerated in an airtight container for up to 5 days. Bring to room temperature before using.

PINEAPPLE-ROASTED PORK SHOULDER

HANDS-ON TIME
30 MIN

TOTAL TIME
3 HRS 45 MIN
PLUS 5 HRS
MARINATING

SERVES 8

The method behind this astonishingly good pork shoulder is one of the best takeaways in this book. I start by roasting a giant bone-in pork roast at 450°F, until it's browned and crisp on the edges. Next, I arrange the parcooked roast on a double layer of heavy-duty foil and drizzle it with a pineapple-based marinade. I wrap it nice and tight and then roast it at 350°F until it's tender. The pork essentially braises in a combination of the marinade and its own juices. The result is a surprisingly easy meal.

2 cups pineapple juice

¼ cup toasted sesame oil

¼ cup low-sodium soy sauce

¼ cup apple cider vinegar

3 garlic cloves, finely grated

3 tablespoons kosher salt

1 (8-pound) bone-in pork shoulder roast

Chopped scallions, for sprinkling

Toasted sesame seeds, for sprinkling

In a 2-gallon resealable plastic bag (you can also use a clean unscented kitchen bag along with a twist tie, if you so choose), whisk together all the ingredients except the pork, scallions, and sesame seeds. Add the pork to the marinade and seal the bag, pressing out as much air as possible. Put the pork in a large baking dish and refrigerate for at least 4 hours or up to overnight. Let the pork sit at room temperature for 1 hour before roasting.

Preheat the oven to 425°F. Line a large rimmed baking sheet with aluminum foil.

Remove the pork from the bag, reserving 1 cup of the marinade. Put the pork on the prepared baking sheet and roast for about 45 minutes, until nicely browned. Remove the pork from the oven and reduce the oven temperature to 350°F.

Lay two very large sheets of heavy-duty foil on a work surface. Put the pork in the center and fold the foil up around the sides, leaving the top open. Pour the reserved marinade over the pork and then wrap it tightly in the foil. Return the pork to the baking sheet and roast for about 2 hours more, until very tender. Let the wrapped pork rest for 30 minutes.

Unwrap the pork and transfer to a carving board. Thinly slice the meat across the grain and transfer to a platter. Pour any accumulated juices on top and sprinkle with chopped scallions and toasted sesame seeds. Serve.

GIANT MEATBALLS

with Marinara Sauce & Parmesan

HANDS-ON TIME
30 MIN

TOTAL TIME
1 HR 15 MIN

SERVES 4 TO 6

Tough meatballs are just so sad. I think the problem is that people tend to overmix the meat while trying to incorporate the other ingredients. I learned to avoid this by using a supersmart method I learned from Sam Mogannam of San Francisco's Bi-Rite Market. It works like a charm! Follow Sam's example and combine all the ingredients except for the meat in a bowl; when that's done, crumble the beef and pork on top before gently mixing everything together.

Extra-virgin olive oil, for greasing

1 large egg, lightly beaten

¾ cup whole-milk ricotta cheese

½ cup plain dry bread crumbs

½ cup finely grated Parmesan cheese, plus more for serving

½ cup finely chopped fresh parsley, plus more for garnish

2 garlic cloves, minced

Kosher salt and freshly ground black pepper

1 pound ground chuck (80% lean)

1 pound ground pork

1 (24-ounce) jar good-quality marinara sauce, such as Rao's

Big green salad, for serving

Preheat the oven to 375°F. Lightly grease a small roasting pan or large baking dish with olive oil.

In a large bowl, beat the egg. Stir in the ricotta, bread crumbs, Parmesan, parsley, garlic, 2 teaspoons salt, and ½ teaspoon pepper. Working over the bowl, break the meat into small chunks. Using your hands, gently toss the mixture until the meat is evenly coated. Using your palms, loosely form the mixture into 6 balls and arrange them in the prepared pan.

Bake the meatballs for about 30 minutes, until an instant-read thermometer inserted into a meatball registers 160°F; rotate the pan halfway through baking. Spoon the marinara sauce over the meatballs and bake for about 10 minutes more, until the sauce is bubbling.

Sprinkle the meatballs with Parmesan and chopped parsley and serve hot, alongside a big green salad.

CLASSIC
MEAT LOAF
SANDWICHES with Tomato Jam

HANDS-ON TIME
20 MIN

TOTAL TIME
1 HR 55 MIN

SERVES 8

Grandma Barbara made meat loaf at least once a week, using a recipe from an enormous cookbook that had been missing its cover since forever. It was one of the first meals I made for myself when I moved to New York City. The only problem was that my roommate, Brandon, didn't eat red meat, so I'd always have a ridiculous amount of leftovers. I learned to not mind, because what better way to use up extras than in a meat loaf sandwich? Nowadays I eat the sandwiches with my homemade tomato jam (page 271), but store-bought ketchup is delicious, too.

2 tablespoons extra-virgin olive oil

1 large onion, finely chopped

6 garlic cloves, minced

   Kosher salt and freshly ground black pepper

2 large eggs, beaten

¾ cup plain dry bread crumbs

½ cup milk

2 tablespoons Worcestershire sauce

2 pounds ground chuck (80% lean)

8 bacon slices (see Tip, opposite)

   Mayonnaise, for spreading

8 slices white country bread, toasted

   Oven-Roasted Tomato Jam (page 271) or ketchup, for serving

   Lettuce, arugula, or watercress, for topping

Preheat the oven to 350°F. Line a large rimmed baking sheet with aluminum foil.

In a large skillet, heat the olive oil over medium-high heat until shimmering. Add the onion, garlic, and a generous pinch each of salt and pepper. Cook, stirring occasionally, until softened and just starting to brown, about 8 minutes. Transfer to a large bowl and let cool.

Add the eggs, bread crumbs, milk, Worcestershire, 1 tablespoon salt, and ½ teaspoon pepper to the onion mixture and mix well. Add the ground beef and mix well. Transfer the meat mixture to the prepared baking sheet and, using damp hands, shape it into a 10 by 5-inch loaf. Drape the bacon slices over the meat loaf on an angle, gently tucking the ends of each slice under the meat loaf.

Bake the meat loaf for about 1 hour 10 minutes, until an instant-read thermometer inserted into the center registers 165°F. Let the meat loaf stand for 10 minutes, then cut crosswise into 1-inch-thick slices.

Spread mayonnaise on each slice of toast. Put a slice of meat loaf on 4 of the toasts. Top with the tomato jam and lettuce. Close the sandwiches and serve right away.

DO IT AHEAD The meat loaf can be refrigerated, covered, for up to 3 days. Reheat in a preheated 350°F oven before serving.

TIP The bacon helps prevent the meat loaf from drying out on top. If you'd rather skip it, just spread some ketchup all over the outside before baking.

LAMB ROAST

with Cheater Harissa, Chickpeas & Kale

HANDS-ON TIME
20 MIN

TOTAL TIME
7 TO 8 HRS ON
LOW OR 4 TO
5 HRS ON HIGH

SERVES 4

One year, someone gave me a huge lamb roast as a holiday gift, which I thought was a super-sweet gesture. I mean, why *not* give someone a leg of lamb? I certainly appreciated it. The only problem was finding the time to roast it. So I decided to let my slow cooker do its thing. I rubbed the lamb with my Cheater Harissa, then set it inside the machine. When it emerged many hours later, it was fantastically tender. Plus, there were plenty of lamb juices left in the slow cooker, so I stirred in a can of chickpeas and a nearly full package of baby kale, and *bam*—a whole dang meal!

1   3- to 3¼-pound boneless lamb shoulder roast

¼   cup Cheater Harissa (page 266), plus more for serving

Kosher salt and freshly ground black pepper

2   (15-ounce) cans chickpeas, drained and rinsed

1   (5-ounce) package baby kale

Rub the lamb shoulder all over with the Cheater Harissa and season with salt and pepper. Roll up the lamb into a neat roast, then tie at 1-inch intervals with kitchen string. Transfer to a slow cooker and add 1 cup water. Cover and cook on Low for 7 to 8 hours or High for 4 to 5 hours, until the lamb is tender.

Transfer the lamb to a carving board and tent with aluminum foil. Stir the chickpeas and kale into the juices in the slow cooker. Cover and let stand until the kale is just wilted, about 5 minutes. Season with salt and pepper.

Carve the lamb across the grain. Ladle the chickpeas, kale, and juices into shallow bowls. Top with the lamb and serve, passing additional harissa at the table.

3-MINUTE STEAKS

with Carrot Chimichurri

TOTAL TIME
20 MIN
SERVES 4

The last time Jason and I went to Paris, we had *steak frites*, like, a million times. Without guilt. The reason? The steaks were far thinner than the gigantic ones served here in the United States. By the time we got back, we vowed to eat smaller steaks. You know, for our health, and maybe a little bit because we Americans enjoy "being French" sometimes more than the French do. Things started out well, but pretty soon we began feeling slightly dissatisfied with our petite meat. The problem was that small steaks cook so quickly, they don't develop a sensational char. So I went on a mission to discover a way to get the crusts we craved. Eventually I figured out that a little cornstarch dusted on the meat before cooking absorbs excess moisture and promotes browning. Now I cook all my "baby steaks" this way, as well as thin-cut pork chops and fish fillets. I love to serve these steaks with a bright, acidic sauce, like my carrot "chimichurri." It's a fun riff on a classic version but with the addition of very thinly sliced pieces of carrots and their greens, which lend a sweetness and earthiness that I find to be downright delicious.

2 small carrots (about 2 ounces), quartered lengthwise and very thinly sliced crosswise

¼ cup finely chopped carrot greens

¼ cup plus 2 tablespoons extra-virgin olive oil

¼ cup finely chopped fresh parsley

3 tablespoons fresh lemon juice

1 garlic clove, finely grated

¼ teaspoon red pepper flakes

Kosher salt and freshly ground black pepper

4 (6-ounce) boneless New York strip steaks, cut ½ inch thick (have your butcher cut them like this)

Cornstarch, for dusting

In a medium bowl, whisk the carrots and their greens with ¼ cup of the olive oil, the parsley, lemon juice, garlic, and red pepper flakes. Season the chimichurri generously with salt and black pepper.

In a large cast-iron skillet (as big as you have!), heat the remaining 2 tablespoons olive oil over high heat until almost smoking. Season the steaks with salt and black pepper. Dust both sides of the steaks with the cornstarch and rub it in with your fingers. Add the steaks to the skillet and cook until crusty on the bottom, about 2 minutes. Flip the steaks and cook until crusty on the other side, 1 minute for medium-rare and 2 minutes for medium.

Transfer the steaks to plates and serve with the carrot chimichurri.

DO IT AHEAD **The carrot chimichurri can be refrigerated in an airtight container overnight. Bring to room temperature before serving.**

3-Minute
STEAKS
with Carrot Chimichurri
PAGE 233

THICK STEAK

with Basil Butter

HANDS-ON TIME
25 MIN

TOTAL TIME
45 MIN

SERVES 4

My friend Paul Nanni is the chef at The Heron, a restaurant near my house in the Catskills. Paul is extraordinarily talented, so you can only imagine how nervous I was when I finally had him over for dinner. I planned to make a big rib-eye steak on the stove in my trusty—and humongous—cast-iron skillet. I got the skillet screaming hot and had the steak searing for only about two minutes before Paul said I should flip it. At this point, I let Paul take over and watched in awe as he flipped the steak over and over, allowing it to cook only a minute or two on each side before turning it again. Then, when the steak was only about halfway done, he took it out of the skillet to rest! After about ten minutes, he popped the meat back in the skillet and continued to cook it, flipping frequently, until it was a perfect medium-rare. Once he cut into it, I could see the perfect reddish-pink color started right at the very top and went all the way to the very bottom, without any gray in between. It was one of the best home-cooked steaks I'd ever had. Now I offer this recipe and that lesson to you.

4 tablespoons (½ stick) unsalted butter, at room temperature or softened in the microwave

2 tablespoons minced fresh basil

1 teaspoon finely grated lemon zest

1 garlic clove, minced

Kosher salt and freshly ground black pepper

1 tablespoon canola oil

1 (1¾-pound) boneless rib-eye steak, cut 2 inches thick

In a bowl, using a fork, blend the butter, basil, lemon zest, and garlic. Season the basil butter generously with salt and pepper.

Preheat a large cast-iron skillet over medium-high heat, then add the canola oil and swirl to coat. Season the steak generously with salt and pepper. Add it to the skillet and cook until lightly browned on the bottom, about 2 minutes. Flip the steak and cook, flipping every 1 to 2 minutes, until an instant-read thermometer inserted into the thickest part registers 65 to 70°F, 6 to 8 minutes. Transfer the steak to a rack set over a baking sheet and let rest for 10 minutes.

Reheat the cast-iron skillet over medium-high heat. Return the steak to the skillet and cook, flipping every minute, until the steak is well browned and an instant-read thermometer inserted into the thickest part registers 120°F, 5 to 7 minutes more. Transfer the steak to a carving board and let rest for 10 minutes. Spread half the basil butter on the steak and carve it across the grain. Spread the remaining basil butter on the sliced steak and serve right away.

DO IT AHEAD The basil butter can be refrigerated in an airtight container for up to 3 days or frozen for 1 month. Bring to room temperature before using.

TIP Compound butter like the basil one in this recipe is a great way to flavor big hunks of meat after they're sliced. I like to spread some of it on the meat just before I carve it, so that tasty butter coats each slice.

DESSERTS & SWEET STUFF

DON'T GET ME WRONG: I LOVE DESSERTS. But I've never put a lot of effort into making them for parties, not because I don't want to but because, well, I forget. By the time I realize my mistake it's too late, so I end up serving ice cream sandwiches, plain cookies, or the store-bought sweets my friends have learned to bring (nothing wrong with that). Still, I've vowed to become a better host by creating some desserts that are so delicious and easy, I'll always remember to make them. Luckily, I've discovered quite a few shortcuts over the years. Some of the strategies—like slicing ice cream right through the paper container to make adorable sandwiches— went viral online because people were blown away by how simple they were. Here I offer new ideas for everything from cheesecake to chocolate mousse.

GLUTEN-FREE
CHOCOLATE-CHERRY
PEANUT BUTTER
COOKIES
240

Chocolate-Peanut
PIE
243

FREE-FORM
APPLE
TART
with Whole Wheat Crust
244

ROCKY ROAD
CLUSTERS
245

DIY Chocolate
TRUFFLES
246

Simplest
CHOCOLATE
MOUSSE
250

Almost-Instant
STRAWBERRY-
VANILLA
ICED CREAM
251

CEREAL MILK
PANNA
COTTA
with Roasted Raspberries
253

NO-BAKE
CHEESECAKE
with Strawberries
254

Salted
BROWNIES
257

ICE CREAM
BIRTHDAY
CAKE
258

HOT CHOCOLATE,
Three Ways

Classic Hot Chocolate 262
Thai-Spiced Hot Chocolate 262
Mexican-Style
Hot Chocolate 263

GLUTEN-FREE CHOCOLATE-CHERRY PEANUT BUTTER COOKIES

HANDS-ON TIME
20 MIN

TOTAL TIME
40 MIN PLUS
COOLING

MAKES ABOUT
24 COOKIES

If you ask me, the best peanut butter cookies are a little chewy and almost raw in the middle, like a Reese's Peanut Butter Cup. When I set out to create my own recipe, that's what I had in mind, and I think I succeeded. But after making these half a dozen times, I realized I wanted *more*. So I poked around the pantry and found some dried cherries. Just like that, Reese's Peanut Butter Cups met peanut butter and jelly. And there ain't nothing wrong with either.

1 cup smooth peanut butter

¾ cup granulated sugar

1 large egg, beaten

¾ teaspoon baking soda

¼ teaspoon kosher salt

½ cup dark chocolate chunks, chopped

½ cup dried cherries, chopped

Position the racks in the upper and lower thirds of the oven and preheat the oven to 350°F. Line two large baking sheets with parchment paper.

In a large bowl, using a wooden spoon, mix the peanut butter, ½ cup of the sugar, the egg, baking soda, and salt. Stir in the chocolate and cherries.

Using a 1-tablespoon measure, scoop heaping tablespoons of the dough onto the prepared baking sheets and then roll them into balls (you should have about 24, depending on how much dough you've snacked on). Dip a fork in the remaining ¼ cup sugar and make a crosshatch pattern on the cookies; dip the fork in sugar before marking each cookie.

Bake the cookies for about 15 minutes, until golden and set; shift the baking sheets from front to back and bottom to top halfway through baking. Let cool for 5 minutes, then transfer to a wire rack to cool completely.

DO IT AHEAD The cookies can be stored in an airtight container at room temperature for up to 3 days.

CHOCOLATE-PEANUT
PIE

HANDS-ON TIME
20 MIN

TOTAL TIME
2 HRS 20 MIN

MAKES ONE
9-INCH PIE

Honey-roasted peanuts are one of my secret addictions. They're just salty-sweet enough and have an irresistible crunch. I've started using them in everything from salads to chocolate desserts. Consider this pie. I mean, how could you not notice my obsession when you see 2 cups of peanuts piled on top of a chocolate ganache? The graham cracker crust comes together in about 15 minutes, but if you're pressed for time, you don't even need to bake it. Or if you're really feeling lazy, you could even make this pie with a store-bought crust.

1½ cups graham cracker crumbs (7 ounces)

½ cup (1 stick) unsalted butter, melted

¼ cup packed light brown sugar

Kosher salt

1⅓ cups heavy cream

1 (12-ounce) bag semisweet chocolate chips

2 cups honey-roasted peanuts

Preheat the oven to 350°F.

In a medium bowl, using a fork, mix the graham cracker crumbs, butter, brown sugar, and ¼ teaspoon salt until evenly moistened. Press the mixture into the bottom and up the side of a 9-inch glass or metal pie plate. Bake the crust for 10 minutes, until lightly browned. Transfer to a wire rack and let cool completely, about 45 minutes.

In a medium saucepan, bring the heavy cream just to a simmer over medium-high heat. Remove from the heat and add the chocolate chips and a pinch of salt. Let stand for 1 minute, then whisk until the ganache is smooth.

Scrape the chocolate ganache into the cooled piecrust and scatter the peanuts evenly on top, gently pressing them into the chocolate. Refrigerate until well chilled, about 1 hour. Cut into wedges and serve.

DO IT AHEAD The pie can be covered with plastic wrap and refrigerated for up to 5 days. If it's been in the refrigerator for a while, let it stand at room temperature for 15 to 20 minutes before slicing.

FREE-FORM
APPLE TART
with Whole Wheat Crust

HANDS-ON TIME
40 MIN

TOTAL TIME
2 HRS 25 MIN
PLUS COOLING

SERVES 8

I learned to make apple tarts at The French Culinary Institute, topping apple compote with gorgeous concentric circles of the most delicate apple slices. When I look back and remember how pretty those tarts were, I also remember how long they took. I no longer have a day to devote to tart-making—more like an hour. So I go for free-form versions with piles of apple and a shortcut compote of apple sauce spiked with grated fresh ginger.

1 cup all-purpose flour, plus more for dusting

½ cup whole wheat flour

¼ cup plus 2 tablespoons sugar, plus more for sprinkling

Kosher salt

10 tablespoons (1¼ sticks) unsalted butter, frozen

⅓ cup very cold water

1 cup applesauce

2 tablespoons peeled and finely grated fresh ginger

3 Granny Smith apples, halved, cored, and thinly sliced

2 tablespoons fresh lemon juice

1 large egg, beaten with 1 tablespoon of water to make an egg wash

In a large bowl, whisk together both flours, 2 tablespoons of the sugar, and ¾ teaspoon salt. Using a box grater, carefully grate the frozen butter over the flour. Using your fingers, toss the butter in the flour until evenly distributed (if the butter softens too quickly, just pop the entire bowl in the freezer for a few minutes). Stir in the cold water until the dough just starts to come together, then turn the dough out onto a work surface and knead a few times until just smooth with streaks of visible butter. Wrap the dough in plastic and refrigerate until chilled, about 45 minutes.

Preheat the oven to 400°F. Line a large rimmed baking sheet with parchment paper.

In a small bowl, whisk the applesauce with the ginger. In a large bowl, toss the apple slices, lemon juice, a pinch of salt, and the remaining ¼ cup sugar.

On a lightly floured work surface, roll out the dough to a 14-inch round and slide it onto the prepared baking sheet. Spread the applesauce over the dough, leaving a 1-inch border. Scatter the apple slices evenly on top of the applesauce. Fold the edge of the dough up and over the apples to create a 1-inch border. Brush the border with the egg wash and sprinkle with sugar.

Bake the tart for about 1 hour, until the crust is nicely browned and the apples are tender. Transfer the pan to a wire rack and let the tart cool. Serve warm or at room temperature.

DO IT AHEAD   The apple tart can be covered with aluminum foil and stored at room temperature for up to 2 days.

ROCKY ROAD CLUSTERS

HANDS-ON TIME
15 MIN

TOTAL TIME
45 MIN

MAKES ABOUT
24 CLUSTERS

I ate lots of Rocky Road ice cream when I was growing up. I didn't always love the nuts, but the little marshmallows more than made up for it. The candy here is my homage, combining mounds of chocolate, marshmallows, and nuts. Plus, talk about easy: These clusters only require toasting some nuts and melting chocolate in the microwave.

2   cups walnut halves
     (8 ounces)

2   cups bittersweet
     chocolate chips
     (10 ounces)

1   cup butterscotch chips
     (5 ounces)

2   tablespoons unsalted
     butter

1   teaspoon pure vanilla
     extract

2   cups mini marshmallows
     (4 ounces)

     Flaky sea salt, such as
     Maldon, for sprinkling

Preheat the oven to 350°F.

Spread the walnuts on a large rimmed baking sheet. Toast in the oven for 8 to 10 minutes, until browned and fragrant. Let cool completely, then coarsely chop. Line the baking sheet with parchment paper.

In a large microwave-safe bowl, combine the chocolate and butterscotch chips and the butter. Microwave on full power in 20-second intervals until almost melted; stir between intervals. Add the vanilla and let stand for 2 minutes, then whisk until smooth. Let cool slightly, then fold in the walnuts and marshmallows.

Scoop 2-tablespoon mounds of the dough onto the prepared baking sheet and sprinkle with flaky sea salt. Refrigerate the Rocky Road clusters until firm, about 30 minutes.

DO IT AHEAD   The Rocky Road clusters can be stored in an airtight container, separated by waxed paper or paper muffin cups, at room temperature for up to 3 days.

DIY CHOCOLATE
TRUFFLES

HANDS-ON TIME
55 MIN

TOTAL TIME
3 HRS 20 MIN

MAKES ABOUT
48 TRUFFLES

Most truffle recipes call for chocolate, heavy cream, and butter. Not that I'm against cream or butter, as you may know by now, but I've discovered that something magical happens when you swap them out for sweetened condensed milk. The milk adds a richness and melt-in-your-mouth texture that's fantastically fudgelike. I opt to coat my truffles in cocoa powder, chopped pistachios, and pearl sugar, but rainbow sprinkles make quite the statement, too.

2 cups bittersweet chocolate chips (10 ounces)

1 (14-ounce) can sweetened condensed milk

1 tablespoon brandy or dark rum

Kosher salt

Unsweetened cocoa powder, for coating

Finely chopped pistachios, for coating

Pearl sugar, for coating

In a medium saucepan, combine the chocolate chips and sweetened condensed milk and cook over medium heat, stirring with a wooden spoon, until the chocolate is just melted, 3 to 5 minutes. Remove from the heat and stir in the brandy and a generous pinch of salt. Scrape into a medium bowl and press a piece of plastic wrap directly against the surface of the chocolate mixture (this prevents it from forming a pesky skin). Let cool and then refrigerate until firm, about 2 hours.

Line a large baking sheet with waxed paper. Place each coating in a separate bowl. Using a 1-tablespoon ice cream scoop or measuring spoon, scoop level mounds of the chocolate mixture onto the baking sheet. One at a time, roll the mounds into balls and then toss in the coatings, pressing gently to help adhere. Transfer the truffles to an airtight container or package in boxes lined with mini-cupcake liners. Refrigerate until chilled, about 30 minutes.

DO IT AHEAD The chocolate truffles can be refrigerated for up to 5 days.

RECIPE CONTINUES

DIY CHOCOLATE
TRUFFLES
PREP

Use a 1-tablespoon scoop to form even mounds.

Scoop the mounds onto a baking sheet lined with waxed paper.

Roll the mounds into perfect balls.

Roll some of the truffles in chopped pistachios, pressing to help adhere.

Toss some of the truffles in crunchy pearl sugar.

Coat some of the truffles in unsweetened cocoa powder.

SIMPLEST CHOCOLATE
MOUSSE

HANDS-ON TIME
30 MIN

TOTAL TIME
1 HR 45 MIN

SERVES 6

The process of making a classic chocolate mousse is enough to make anyone, amateur or expert, a little twitchy. It starts with a chocolaty egg custard, which, in and of itself, is notoriously finicky. The eggs can scramble or make the base lumpy, while the chocolate can easily seize if it gets too hot. Then you fold in whipped cream. This step also makes me nervous, even with all my years of practice, because overmixing will quickly deflate your mousse.

But there's an easier way to make mousse, and I'm sharing it with you. Rather than starting with a custard base, I just melt chocolate in hot heavy cream. Then I whisk in cocoa powder to make it intensely chocolaty, and espresso powder, which adds lots of personality. Once the chocolate cream cools, I tuck it into the refrigerator until it's well chilled. But here's the genius part: I whip the chilled chocolate cream until just stiff. Done!

2½ cups heavy cream

1 cup milk chocolate chips (5 ounces)

2 tablespoons unsweetened cocoa powder

1 teaspoon instant espresso powder

½ teaspoon kosher salt

½ teaspoon pure vanilla extract

Shaved or grated chocolate, for sprinkling

In a medium saucepan, bring 2 cups of the heavy cream just to a simmer over medium-high heat. Remove from the heat and add the chocolate chips. Let stand for 2 minutes, then whisk until smooth. Whisk in the cocoa powder, instant espresso, and salt. Transfer the chocolate cream to a large bowl and let cool completely. Cover with plastic wrap and refrigerate until chilled, about 1 hour.

Using a handheld mixer, beat the chocolate cream until smooth and holds stiff peaks when you lift the beater out of the bowl. Do not overbeat the cream because the fat will begin to separate and it'll look curdled (see Note)—you're making mousse, not butter! Spoon the chocolate mousse into bowls or glasses and refrigerate until ready to serve.

In another large bowl, using the handheld mixer, beat the remaining ½ cup heavy cream with the vanilla until smooth and holds a soft peak when you lift the beater out of the bowl. Spoon the whipped cream on top of the chocolate mousse and sprinkle with shaved or grated chocolate. Serve cold.

NOTE If you happen to whip the cream a little too much, very gently fold in cold heavy cream, 1 tablespoon at a time, until the mixture is creamy again.

DO IT AHEAD The chocolate mousse can be refrigerated, covered, for up to 2 days.

ALMOST-INSTANT STRAWBERRY-VANILLA ICED CREAM

HANDS-ON TIME
30 MIN

TOTAL TIME
6 HR 30 MIN

MAKES 1 QUART

Ice cream is probably my greatest weakness. When I was growing up, Grandma Barbara would buy giant tubs of it that were so heavy, they came with their own handles. My favorite flavor, then and now, is strawberry. Even when the flavor is artificial, like Strawberry Quik, I devour it.

Since I've gotten older and become kind of a good cook (insert dimpled smile), I really like to make ice cream at home. I've tried all sorts of ambitious recipes, including salted caramel–rosemary, but I always go back to strawberry. One summer while up at my house in the Catskills (yep, where *Dirty Dancing* took place) I was craving it real bad but didn't have an ice cream maker on hand. I didn't have eggs, either. That's when I came up with this almost-instant version. The secret is whipping heavy cream with just a tiny bit of unflavored gelatin, which helps stabilize it, and then folding it into sweetened condensed milk laced with strawberry jam. It's not exactly ice cream, which is why I call it "iced cream." Whatever—it's delicious.

1 (14-ounce) can sweetened condensed milk

½ cup Strawberry-Lemon Quick Jam (page 274) or store-bought strawberry preserves

½ vanilla bean, split and seeds scraped, or ½ teaspoon pure vanilla extract

¼ teaspoon kosher salt

1 teaspoon unflavored powdered gelatin

2 cups heavy cream

DO IT AHEAD The iced cream can be frozen for up to 2 weeks.

Put a 9 by 5-inch metal loaf pan in the freezer to chill.

In a large bowl, whisk together the sweetened condensed milk, strawberry preserves, vanilla seeds, and salt. Refrigerate until chilled, about 15 minutes.

In a small saucepan, sprinkle the gelatin over 3 tablespoons water. Let stand until nearly dissolved, about 3 minutes. Bring the mixture to a simmer over medium heat, stirring until the gelatin is completely dissolved. Scrape into a large bowl and let cool slightly.

Add the heavy cream to the bowl with the gelatin and, using a handheld mixer, beat on medium-high speed until the cream holds stiff peaks, about 2 minutes. Do not overbeat the cream because the fat will begin to separate and it will look curdled (see Note, page 250).

Using a rubber spatula, stir one-third of the whipped cream into the condensed milk mixture to lighten it. Fold in the remaining whipped cream by scooping cream from the bottom of the bowl and folding it over the top with the rubber spatula; rotate the bowl occasionally while folding. Scrape the strawberry cream into the chilled loaf pan. Cover with plastic wrap and freeze until firm, about 6 hours. Serve in bowls or glasses, or on an ice cream cone.

CEREAL MILK PANNA COTTA

with Roasted Raspberries

HANDS-ON TIME
15 MIN

TOTAL TIME
2 HRS 15 MIN

SERVES 4

Believe it or not, I keep unflavored powdered gelatin on hand at all times. It's one of those wonky ingredients that home cooks tend to be afraid of, even though there's nothing scary about it. The directions are printed right on the box! Okay, enough ranting, because I'm sure after making these panna cottas, you'll understand why I use gelatin so often. Here it transforms almond milk into a delicate custard. Oh, and about the name of this recipe: The combo of almond milk and honey tastes a lot like those last drops of milk at the bottom of a bowl of Honey Nut Cheerios.

1½	teaspoons unflavored powdered gelatin
2	cups vanilla almond milk
4	tablespoons granulated sugar
2	tablespoons honey
	Kosher salt
½	pint raspberries

In a small bowl, sprinkle the gelatin over ½ cup of the almond milk and let stand until nearly dissolved, about 3 minutes.

In a medium saucepan, combine the remaining 1½ cups almond milk, 3 tablespoons sugar, honey, and a pinch of salt. Bring just to a simmer over medium-high heat, stirring to dissolve the sugar. Remove from the heat and whisk in the gelatin mixture until completely dissolved. Spoon any foam off the top of the panna cotta mixture, then pour into 5- to 6-ounce glasses. Let cool slightly and then cover the glasses with plastic wrap. Refrigerate until set and chilled, about 2 hours.

Preheat the oven to 400°F.

On a rimmed baking sheet, toss the raspberries with the remaining 1 tablespoon sugar and a pinch of salt. Roast for about 10 minutes, until just juicy. Let cool completely.

Spoon the cooled roasted raspberries onto the panna cottas and serve chilled.

DO IT AHEAD The panna cottas can be refrigerated, covered, overnight (just don't make the raspberries until the day you're serving them).

NO-BAKE
CHEESECAKE

with Strawberries

HANDS-ON TIME
30 MIN

TOTAL TIME
4 HRS 30 MIN

MAKES ONE
9-INCH CAKE

Everything about this cheesecake is brilliant—and no-bake! Crumbled Oreo cookies (cream and all) and a little bit of melted butter come together to form a crust that hardens when chilled. The cream-cheese-and-ricotta filling also sets up in the freezer while staying light and super creamy. I like to top the cheesecake with sugared strawberries, but if you're a real cookie monster, you could just sprinkle on some coarsely crushed Oreos, too.

24	Oreos or other cream-filled wafer sandwich cookies (9 ounces)
4	tablespoons (½ stick) unsalted butter, melted
2	(8-ounce) packages cream cheese, at room temperature
1	pound whole-milk ricotta
¼	cup honey or light agave nectar
2	tablespoons sugar
	Kosher salt
2	cups strawberries (12 ounces), hulled and quartered (see Tip)
1	tablespoon fresh lemon juice

In a food processor, pulse the cookies until finely ground. Add the butter and pulse until the crumbs are evenly moistened. Transfer the crumbs to a 9-inch springform pan and press them evenly over the bottom and ½ inch up the sides. Cover with plastic wrap and refrigerate until chilled, about 30 minutes.

Meanwhile, clean the bowl of the food processor. Add the cream cheese, ricotta, honey, 1 tablespoon of the sugar, and ¼ teaspoon salt and puree until smooth (you can also do this in a large bowl using a handheld mixer, but it might be a little less smooth). Scrape the filling into the chilled crust and, using an offset spatula, spread the filling evenly and smooth the top. Cover with plastic wrap and freeze until firm, about 1 hour.

In a large bowl, toss the strawberries with the lemon juice and the remaining 1 tablespoon sugar. Let stand, stirring occasionally, until very juicy, about 1 hour.

Unmold the cheesecake and transfer to a platter. Cut into wedges and serve with the strawberries.

DO IT AHEAD The cheesecake can be refrigerated, covered, for up to 5 days. The strawberries can be refrigerated in an airtight container for up to 2 days.

TIP Save as much of the strawberry as you can by hulling it with a straw. Insert a plastic drinking straw into the bottom of the strawberry and push it toward the top, releasing the hull.

SALTED BROWNIES

HANDS-ON TIME
15 MIN

TOTAL TIME
1 HR PLUS
COOLING

SERVES 8

Not that you couldn't happily eat these brownies all on their own, but I have the most fun figuring out how to incorporate them into other desserts. For instance, I tuck them into my Ice Cream Birthday Cake (page 258), layer them with pudding to make trifles, and even mash them up with frosting and mold them onto sticks to make cake pops. So get creative!

¾ cup (1½ sticks) unsalted butter

1 (12-ounce) bag semisweet chocolate chips

1 cup sugar

3 large eggs

¾ cup all-purpose flour

1 tablespoon pure vanilla extract

1½ teaspoons baking powder

¾ teaspoon flaky sea salt, such as Maldon, plus more for sprinkling

Preheat the oven to 350°F. Line the bottom and two sides of an 8-inch square metal baking pan with aluminum foil, allowing 2 inches of overhang on the two sides.

In a medium saucepan, melt the butter and chocolate chips over low heat, stirring occasionally, until smooth, about 5 minutes. Let cool slightly, then whisk in the sugar, eggs, flour, vanilla, baking powder, and flaky sea salt until smooth. Scrape the batter into the prepared pan and smooth the top.

Bake the brownies for 40 to 45 minutes, until a toothpick inserted into the center comes out with a few moist crumbs attached. Sprinkle the brownies with flaky sea salt and then let cool completely, about 1 hour. Lift the brownies out of the pan and peel off the foil. Cut the brownies into bars and serve.

DO IT AHEAD The brownies can be stored at room temperature, covered, or refrigerated in an airtight container for up to 5 days.

ICE CREAM BIRTHDAY CAKE

HANDS-ON TIME
1 HR

TOTAL TIME
AT LEAST
10 HRS

SERVES 8

As a kid, I'd stare into the freezer at Baskin-Robbins and dream of having the party cake covered in "clown cones." This recipe is my grown-up version. It's five layers of my favorite flavors—vanilla and strawberry—and salty brownies.

Salted Brownies (page 257), or 1 (8-inch) square package large brownies

1 pint vanilla ice cream, softened slightly

1 pint strawberry ice cream, softened slightly

1½ cups heavy cream

2 tablespoons confectioners' sugar

½ teaspoon pure vanilla extract

Crushed nuts, sprinkles, maraschino cherries, or candies, for decorating

Line the bottom and the two long sides of a 9 by 5-inch loaf pan with aluminum foil, allowing 2 inches of overhang on the two long sides. Place a serving platter for the cake in the refrigerator to chill.

Using a serrated knife, cut the brownies in half crosswise to create thinner slabs. Arrange a layer of brownie slabs in the bottom of the prepared pan, cutting them to fit snugly if necessary. Spread the vanilla ice cream over the brownie layer and smooth the top. Arrange another layer of brownies over the vanilla ice cream, gently pressing them to help them adhere to the ice cream. Spread the strawberry ice cream over the brownies. Arrange a final layer of brownies over the strawberry ice cream. Freeze the cake until very firm, about 3 hours.

In a large bowl, using a handheld mixer, beat the heavy cream, confectioners' sugar, and vanilla until stiff peaks form.

Working quickly, using the foil as handles, lift the ice cream cake out of the pan and invert it onto the chilled platter; peel off the foil. Decoratively spread the whipped cream all over the cake and decorate with whatever toppings you choose. Freeze the cake until very firm, at least 6 hours or up to overnight. To serve, cut the cake into slices and transfer to plates.

DO IT AHEAD Once frozen, the ice cream cake can be covered with plastic and kept in the freezer for up to 1 week.

HOT CHOCOLATE,
THREE WAYS

I think people have trouble distinguishing between hot chocolate from a mix and the real kind: warm milk whisked with melted chocolate chips until rich and silky. I also think people forget (or maybe even never knew) how quickly real hot chocolate comes together. Here, a few versions that will take you around the world one mug at a time.

RECIPE CONTINUES

CLASSIC HOT CHOCOLATE

TOTAL TIME 15 MIN / SERVES 4

- 3 cups whole milk
- ⅓ cup sugar
- Pinch of kosher salt
- 1½ cups bittersweet chocolate chips (about 8 ounces)
- ½ teaspoon pure vanilla extract
- Whipped cream or marshmallows, for serving
- Finely grated chocolate, for topping

In a medium saucepan, combine the milk, sugar, and salt and bring just to a simmer over medium heat, stirring to dissolve the sugar. Remove from the heat and add the chocolate. Let stand for 2 minutes, then add the vanilla and stir until smooth. Pour the hot chocolate into mugs and serve with whipped cream or marshmallows, topped with grated chocolate.

THAI-SPICED HOT CHOCOLATE

TOTAL TIME 15 MIN / SERVES 4

- 2 cups whole milk
- 1 (14-ounce) can unsweetened coconut milk
- ⅓ cup sugar
- 1½ teaspoons ground cinnamon
- ¼ teaspoon ground cardamom
- ⅛ teaspoon ground cloves
- Pinch of kosher salt
- 1½ cups bittersweet chocolate chips (about 8 ounces)
- Whipped cream and marshmallows, for topping

In a medium saucepan, combine the milk, coconut milk, sugar, cinnamon, cardamom, cloves, and salt. Bring just to a simmer over medium heat, stirring to dissolve the sugar. Remove from the heat and add the chocolate. Let stand for 2 minutes, then stir until smooth. Pour the hot chocolate into mugs, top with whipped cream or marshmallows, and serve.

MEXICAN-STYLE HOT CHOCOLATE

TOTAL TIME 15 MIN / SERVES 4

3	cups whole milk
⅓	cup packed light brown sugar
2	teaspoons ground cinnamon
¼	teaspoon cayenne pepper
	Pinch of kosher salt
1½	cups bittersweet chocolate chips (about 8 ounces)
1	teaspoon pure vanilla extract
	Whipped cream or marshmallows, for topping

In a medium saucepan, combine the milk, brown sugar, cinnamon, cayenne, and salt and bring just to a simmer over medium heat, stirring to dissolve the sugar. Remove from the heat and add the chocolate. Let stand for 2 minutes, then add the vanilla and stir until smooth. Pour the hot chocolate into mugs, top with whipped cream or marshmallows, and serve.

CONDIMENTS & SAUCES

I'M NOT SURE ABOUT YOU, but I've spent a fortune on small-batch hot sauces, fancy jams, artisanal pickles, and the like, and devoted hours to coming up with my own DIY versions. What I've found is that the best do more than just add a little bit of heat, tang, or sweetness to an otherwise basic dish: They elevate the experience to a whole other level. A sprinkle of my Pistachio-Almond Dukka, with its mix of Middle Eastern seeds and spices, transforms ricotta gnudi (page 173). And while my strawberry jam is very nice on toast, it does something truly exciting to ice cream (page 251). I hope you'll be inspired by all the ways I use condiments and sauces throughout the book and come up with a few ideas of your own along the way.

Cheater
HARISSA
266

SPEEDY
PRESERVED LEMONS
267

AVOCADO
MAYO
268

BBQ Sauce
VINAIGRETTE
269

Oven-Roasted
TOMATO JAM
271

QUICK-PICKLED
RED ONIONS
272

Strawberry-Lemon
QUICK JAM
274

All-Purpose
BUTTERMILK RANCH
275

QUICK
KIRBY PICKLES
with Ginger & Jalapeño
277

Pickled-Pepper
ROUILLE
278

DRIED
HERB OIL
279

Pistachio-Almond
DUKKA
280

ALL-PURPOSE LEMONY
BREAD CRUMBS
281

CHEATER HARISSA

Harissa is a North African chile paste that's terrific with pretty much anything, especially grassy cuts of meat like lamb. You can buy it in a lot of grocery stores nowadays but somehow, when I *really* need it, it's nowhere to be found. That's why I keep this cheater version close by. Paprika, garlic, cumin, and coriander give it incredible depth, while chipotles chiles in adobo (my untraditional addition) provide smokiness and heat. I like my harissa pretty loose so I can use it as a dip or spread, but just add a little less oil if you want a thicker paste.

3   tablespoons sweet smoked paprika

3   tablespoons fresh lemon juice

2   canned chipotles in adobo, seeded and minced

2   garlic cloves, minced

2   teaspoons kosher salt

¾   teaspoon ground cumin

¾   teaspoon ground coriander

¼   cup extra-virgin olive oil

In a small bowl, whisk everything except the olive oil together until smooth. Gradually whisk in the olive oil until incorporated. Scrape into a jar, cover, and refrigerate until chilled.

DO IT AHEAD   The harissa can be refrigerated for up to 5 days.

SPEEDY
PRESERVED
LEMONS

HANDS-ON TIME
10 MIN

TOTAL TIME
25 MIN PLUS
COOLING

MAKES 1 PINT

Preserved lemons can take up to a month to make using the traditional technique of salting the citrus and packing it tightly in a jar. Over time, the peels get super tender and can be cut off the pith and used in sauces or stews, or even salads (see my grain salad on page 165). My speedy version just requires about 10 minutes of simmering in salted water, which softens the peels and concentrates the flavor. It's such a great hack that I rarely ever make—or buy—traditional preserved lemons anymore.

4 Meyer or thin-skinned lemons, scrubbed and cut into 6 wedges

3 tablespoons kosher salt

In a medium saucepan, combine the lemon wedges, salt, and 2 cups water. Bring to a boil over high heat, then simmer over medium heat until the lemon peels are very tender, about 10 minutes. Let cool completely.

Using a slotted spoon, transfer the lemons to a 1-pint jar with a tight-fitting lid. Pour in just enough of the cooking liquid to cover the lemons. Seal the jar and store in the refrigerator for up to 6 months.

HOW TO USE Using a thin knife, scrape off and discard the lemon pulp and the bitter white pith, then thinly slice or mince the peel. Mix into salad dressings or meat marinades, or use as a condiment to grilled or roasted meats and vegetables.

AVOCADO MAYO

HANDS-ON TIME
10 MIN

TOTAL TIME
30 MIN

MAKES 1½
CUPS

Mayonnaise might be my favorite condiment, but I have a lot of friends who truly dislike it, so I started keeping store-bought substitutes in my fridge. Then one day I remembered something my friend Kate told me: When her kids, Cole and Claire, were little, they refused to eat mayo, so she'd add mashed avocado to their sandwiches instead. That's the inspiration for my avocado mayo. It's luscious, it's tasty, and it's far healthier than mayonnaise. I store it in the fridge in a plastic container with a lid, where it'll keep for almost a week. It's great spread on sandwiches or rye crisps topped with pickled vegetables, or even mixed into canned tuna fish.

2 Hass avocados, halved and pitted

2 tablespoons champagne vinegar

2 teaspoons Dijon mustard

⅓ cup extra-virgin olive oil

Kosher salt

Using a spoon, scoop the avocado into a blender or food processor. Add the vinegar and mustard and puree until nearly smooth. With the machine running, drizzle in the olive oil until incorporated and the avocado mayo is smooth. Scrape into a bowl or jar and season with salt. Cover and refrigerate until thickened and chilled, about 30 minutes.

DO IT AHEAD The avocado mayo can be refrigerated for up to 5 days.

BBQ SAUCE
VINAIGRETTE

HANDS-ON TIME
10 MIN

TOTAL TIME
30 MIN

MAKES 1½
CUPS

I've made this recipe probably more than any I've ever created, but I still get excited even just *thinking* about it. The trick is doctoring store-bought BBQ sauce, which might sound bizarre but is my all-time favorite hack. It's great for salads, like my Grilled Broccolini and Escarole Salad (page 113), makes an awesome glaze for baked chicken wings, and is the ultimate mop sauce for ribs and burgers.

1 cup store-bought plain barbecue sauce

¼ cup extra-virgin olive oil

¼ cup apple cider vinegar

1 garlic clove, minced or finely grated

Kosher salt and freshly ground black pepper

In a medium bowl, whisk together the barbecue sauce, olive oil, vinegar, and garlic. Season the vinaigrette generously with salt and pepper. Refrigerate until chilled, about 20 minutes.

DO IT AHEAD **The BBQ Sauce Vinaigrette can be refrigerated for up to 2 weeks.**

OVEN-ROASTED TOMATO JAM

HANDS-ON TIME
15 MIN

TOTAL TIME
1 HR 15 MIN
PLUS COOLING

MAKES 1½ CUPS

Ketchup most certainly has a place in every kitchen, but I love tomato jam even more, for a couple of reasons: It's not as sweet and it's a cinch to make in the oven. I flavor my basic jam with just some red wine vinegar and spicy red pepper flakes, though sometimes I add fennel or mustard seeds to boost the flavor and lend a little more texture. As you'll see, it's easy to customize the recipe to your own tastes.

2 pounds plum tomatoes, cored and cut into 1-inch pieces

½ cup packed light brown sugar

¼ cup red wine vinegar

1 tablespoon kosher salt

½ teaspoon red pepper flakes

Preheat the oven to 425°F.

In a 9 by 13-inch ceramic baking dish, combine all the ingredients and mix well. Roast, stirring two or three times, for about 1 hour, until the tomatoes break down and are coated in a light syrup.

Using a potato masher or fork, smash the tomato mixture into a coarse paste. Let the jam cool completely, then transfer to a 1-pint glass jar with a tight-fitting lid. Refrigerate until chilled.

DO IT AHEAD The tomato jam can be refrigerated for up to 3 weeks.

QUICK-PICKLED RED ONIONS

HANDS-ON TIME
10 MIN

TOTAL TIME
1 HR 10 MIN

MAKES 1 PINT

Pickled onions can turn anyone into a DIY food artisan—they're so easy and so fun. Just make your pickle brine by shaking everything in a jar, then add thinly sliced red onions and let them hang out for a bit in the refrigerator. In one hour they become tangy and crisp with an outstanding pink color. I love them with my Oven-Fried Pork Carnitas (page 223), but every year around the holidays I serve them with chopped liver and crackers. They're also wonderful in holiday salads, like escarole served with my All-Purpose Buttermilk Ranch (page 275).

¾ cup distilled white vinegar

2 teaspoons kosher salt

2 teaspoons granulated sugar

1 small red onion, halved and very thinly sliced

Combine the vinegar, salt, sugar, and ¼ cup water in a 1-pint jar or plastic container with a tight-fitting lid. Close the jar and shake vigorously to dissolve the salt and sugar. Add the onion, close the jar, and shake to mix. Refrigerate for 1 hour. Take them out of the brine before serving.

DO IT AHEAD The pickled onions can be refrigerated in the brine for up to 2 weeks.

STRAWBERRY-LEMON
QUICK JAM

TOTAL TIME
20 MIN

MAKES 2 CUPS

Jams and jellies aren't necessarily difficult to make, but I think we all shudder at the thought of sterilizing all those jars and lids for canning. Which is why, most of the time, I opt for quick jam. Not only is it, well, quick, but it doesn't require any store-bought pectin. Plus, it's easy to prepare on a regular basis. I make small batches of jam that I always use up before it starts to go bad. I guarantee you'll go through your own batches just as fast.

1½ pounds ripe strawberries, hulled and quartered (see Tip, page 254)

½ cup sugar

1 teaspoon finely grated lemon zest

¼ cup fresh lemon juice

¼ teaspoon kosher salt

In a large nonstick skillet, combine all the ingredients. Cook over medium-high heat, mashing the strawberries with a wooden spoon, until the juices start to release, about 5 minutes. Cook, stirring frequently, until the jam is thickened, 3 to 5 minutes more. It will look like very small chunks of strawberries coated in a thick syrup. Let cool slightly, stirring occasionally, then transfer to a heatproof container to cool completely. Cover and refrigerate until well chilled, about 1 hour.

DO IT AHEAD The strawberry jam can be refrigerated in an airtight container for up to 2 weeks.

ALL-PURPOSE
BUTTERMILK RANCH

HANDS-ON TIME
10 MIN

TOTAL TIME
30 MIN

MAKES 1¼ CUPS

I'm not ashamed to say I still use bottled ranch every now and then, but my homemade version is way healthier because it doesn't have all the sugar and preservatives. The secret to getting that classic flavor are garlic and onion powders, which I happen to think are flavor bombs, even though some cooks frown on them. I love this dressing on my Beans & Peas salad (page 116) and, best of all, drizzled on pizza. Don't knock it till you try it!

½ cup buttermilk

½ cup mayonnaise

1 tablespoon minced chives

1 tablespoon minced fresh dill

¾ teaspoon garlic powder

¾ teaspoon onion powder

Kosher salt and freshly ground black pepper

In a medium bowl, whisk together the buttermilk, mayonnaise, chives, dill, garlic powder, and onion powder. Season the ranch with salt and pepper. Use immediately or cover and refrigerate until ready to use.

DO IT AHEAD The ranch dressing can be refrigerated in an airtight container for up to 3 days.

QUICK KIRBY PICKLES

with Ginger & Jalapeño

HANDS-ON TIME
10 MIN

TOTAL TIME
2 HRS 30 MIN

MAKES 1 QUART

Can you boil water? Then you can make pickles. Just follow the proportions for packing the cukes and prepping the brine—everything from the vinegar to the salt—then add whatever flavorings you want. It could be ginger and jalapeño (as in this recipe), or dill, cumin, parley, chipotle . . . you name it. This, my friends, is one of those recipes you'll make your own, tweaking it over time, until one day you'll forget who got you started in the first place.

¾ cup unseasoned rice vinegar

2½ tablespoons sugar

1 tablespoon kosher salt

1 jalapeño, halved lengthwise

1 (3-inch) piece peeled fresh ginger, sliced crosswise, and lightly crushed

1 pound kirby cucumbers, cut lengthwise into ¾-inch wedges

In a medium saucepan, combine the vinegar, sugar, salt, jalapeño, ginger, and ¾ cup water. Bring to a boil over high heat, stirring to dissolve the sugar and salt. Transfer the brine to a 1-quart heatproof glass or plastic container. Pack the cucumber wedges in the brine and let cool completely, then refrigerate for 2 hours before serving.

DO IT AHEAD   The pickles can be refrigerated for up to 2 weeks.

PICKLED-PEPPER
ROUILLE

HANDS-ON TIME
10 MIN

TOTAL TIME
25 MIN

MAKES ABOUT
1 CUP

When it comes to *rouille* (the classic French sauce traditionally served alongside bouillabaisse), there seem to be many versions that claim to be *the* classic. Some call for copious amounts of olive oil; others are mostly bread, either fresh or in crumb form. I'm happy every time I make my own highly personal variation because not only is it silky and pleasantly garlicky, but it's got pickled hot cherry peppers. It's great with fish stew (page 98), as you'd expect, but it also makes a sensational addition to a BLT.

1 cup mayonnaise

1 pickled hot red cherry pepper, seeded and chopped

2 tablespoons panko bread crumbs

1 tablespoon fresh lemon juice

1 garlic clove, crushed

   Kosher salt

In a mini food processor or a blender, combine the mayonnaise, hot pepper, panko, lemon juice, and garlic and puree until thick and smooth. Scrape into a small bowl and season with salt. Cover and refrigerate for 15 minutes.

DO IT AHEAD   The rouille can be refrigerated in an airtight container for up to 3 days.

DRIED
HERB OIL

HANDS-ON TIME
10 MIN

TOTAL TIME
40 MIN

MAKES 1 CUP

This recipe is a spin-off of a dried-herb dip that Jason has made, somewhat sheepishly, for years. He thinks it's the silliest thing ever but I've always loved it—we even bought a special bowl for it. I'll convince him at some point to let me publish his recipe, but in the meantime, I've made my own variation. I infuse fruity olive oil with herbs, like bay and rosemary and oregano, then drizzle it on creamy feta dip (page 36). I think it's a great dip for bread, too. Be sure to tell Jason if you agree.

1 cup extra-virgin olive oil

4 dried bay leaves, crumbled and minced

2 teaspoons dried oregano, rubbed

2 teaspoons crushed dried rosemary

1 teaspoon red pepper flakes

Kosher salt and freshly ground black pepper

In a small jar or plastic container with a tight-fitting lid, combine the olive oil, bay leaves, oregano, rosemary, and red pepper flakes, then shake well. Season the dried herb oil generously with salt and black pepper. Shake again and let stand at room temperature for 30 minutes before using.

DO IT AHEAD The dried herb oil can be stored in an airtight container at room temperature for up to 1 month. Shake it up before using.

PISTACHIO-ALMOND
DUKKA

HANDS-ON TIME
20 MIN

TOTAL TIME
30 MIN

MAKES 1½
CUPS

Dukka, which gets its name from the Arabic for "to pound," is made of spices, seeds, and nuts ground into a distinctive, aromatic condiment traditionally served with bread and olive oil. I became infatuated with it when a friend brought back a little container from Egypt. I'd had dukka before, but that batch was so flavorful that I couldn't stop thinking about new ways to use it. Sure, I sprinkled it all over olive oil–soaked bread, but then I got the genius idea to shower it over pasta, and then my homemade gnudi (page 173). To get started, try it on ricotta toast with a drizzle of honey . . . yum!

¼ cup coriander seeds

2 tablespoons cumin seeds

2 tablespoons sesame seeds

1 teaspoon caraway seeds

½ cup shelled pistachios (salted or not)

½ cup roasted almonds (salted or not)

¼ teaspoon cayenne pepper

Kosher salt and freshly ground black pepper

In a large skillet, toast the coriander, cumin, sesame, and caraway seeds over medium heat, shaking the pan, until fragrant and the sesame seeds are golden, 5 to 7 minutes. Transfer the seed mixture to a plate to cool.

Transfer the seed mixture to a food processor and pulse until finely crushed. Add the pistachios and almonds and pulse until the nuts are finely ground. Transfer to a jar or other container with a lid. Stir in the cayenne and season the dukka generously with salt and black pepper.

DO IT AHEAD The dukka can be stored in an airtight container at room temperature for up to 1 month.

ALL-PURPOSE LEMONY
BREAD CRUMBS

TOTAL TIME
15 MIN

MAKES 1 CUP

I reach for these bread crumbs all the time. They're my secret weapon for fixing a recipe that's a little too simple, or adding texture to a dish that really needs it. I sprinkle them on everything from my All-Day Cassoulet (page 107) to roasted cauliflower and sautéed green beans. They're especially useful during the holidays, like Thanksgiving and Christmas, when you can shower them on basic steamed veggies to make them entertaining-worthy. This recipe makes 1 cup, which is enough for quite a few uses, so I'd say keep them in an airtight container for a few days or just make a half batch. Whatever you do, don't think too hard about it. Just cook it!

1½ tablespoons extra-virgin olive oil

1 cup panko bread crumbs

1 lemon

Kosher salt and freshly ground black pepper

2 tablespoons minced fresh parsley

In a large nonstick skillet, heat the olive oil over medium-high heat until shimmering. Add the bread crumbs and cook, stirring or tossing frequently, until golden, about 5 minutes. Transfer to a medium bowl and, using a fine grater, grate the zest of the lemon on top. Season with salt and pepper and mix well. Let cool, then stir in the parsley.

DO IT AHEAD The lemony bread crumbs can be stored in an airtight container at room temperature for up to 3 days. You can add the parsley whenever, but the leaves will stay bright green if you stir them in just before using them—something to remember if you're entertaining.

ACKNOWLEDGMENTS

It's impossible to name all of the people who have influenced my career as a cook. I can't begin to express my gratitude to the countless chefs, writers, and home cooks who have inspired so many of my recipes, or to the family and friends who have served me meals I can only dream of replicating. I've learned so much from so many, and I'm forever grateful.

To my agent, Stacey Glick: Can you believe it? It seems like forever ago that we first started pulling this project together. Thank you for the incredible support and guidance throughout this entire process. I literally could not have done this without you. You're an amazing agent and friend!

To Justin Schwartz: Thank you for believing in me as an author long before so many others. You're a brilliant editor, and it's been an absolute pleasure working with you on this book. And thank you to the entire Houghton Mifflin Harcourt team—you're all masters in this field!

One of the best times of my life was the week we spent shooting this book. Who knew you could have so much fun at work? I owe it to the entire shoot team. Thank you, David Malosh. You are an unassumingly brilliant photographer! Thank you for everything from your beautiful photos to your stellar breakfasts. Thank you to Ayesha Patel—your ability to tell stories with props is nothing short of impressive. You knew exactly what I loved without me saying a word. Thank you to my friend and favorite food stylist in the world, Barrett Washburne. I love and appreciate each and every time I get to work with you. And to Mark Anthony Vasquez, thank you for all your hard work and outstanding playlists. Barrett is lucky to have you.

I wouldn't be where I am today if it weren't for my *Food & Wine* family. First, thank you to Christina Grdovic and Diella Koberstein Allen for taking a chance on a quirky little line cook with big dreams. (Love this job, love this team!) Thank you to Dana Cowin for recognizing my talents even when I couldn't. As if your constant support and expert guidance weren't enough, you even brought out the "mad genius" in me.

To Tina Ujlaki: Thank you for being one of the best mentors anyone could ask for. You'll never know all the ways you've impacted my life or how much I've learned from you.

To Kate Heddings: Eight years ago you interviewed me in a tiny conference room . . . and look at us now! Thank you for being one of my dearest friends. Your guidance has made me a better worker, but it's your friendship that has changed my life immeasurably. I cannot express in just these few short sentences what you mean to me. I'll try harder over a rum and Diet Coke.

Many thanks to all the other *Food & Wine* folks who've taught me so much and made work insanely fun: Kristin Donnelly, Mary Ellen Ward, Pam Kaufman, Ray Isle, Christine Quinlan, Daniel Gritzer, Marcia Kiesel, Grace Parisi, Kay Chun, Emily Tylman, David McCann, Julia Heffelfinger, Kate Krader, Maggie Mariolis, Anna Painter, Susan Choung, Lisa Leventer, Kelsey Youngman, and Laura Rege.

I'm one of the luckiest guys when it comes to friends. You all know who you are, and I hope you know how thankful I am to have you in my life. I'm especially grateful to Brandon Davis —you've been my sidekick for nearly twenty years, and I love you for it.

A huge part of who I am today is because of my humongous family. Thank you all! I'm especially thankful for Grandma Barbara, who sacrificed so much to make my childhood a better one. Thank you to my mom and dad, Toni and Mark, for loving me regardless of my choices. Thank you, Aunt Susie and Uncle Don. You've always treated me like one of your own, and I can only try to pay that forward.

Thank you to all of my amazing siblings and cousin-brothers, who taught me everything from how not to trim my bangs to how to make the perfect red rice: Heather, Amanda, Megan, Kevin, Travis, and Kenny. I love you all more than I could ever express.

Thank you to the entire Sarnoff family for welcoming me into your life with open arms—especially Joel, Rena, and Melissa. Joel, your spunk is incredible and you are wittier than anyone I've ever met.

Plus, a special thank-you to all my little nieces and nephews—from California to Maryland—who continuously make me feel famous.

Finally, thank you to Jason: You are my biggest fan and strongest champion. You make me laugh louder and cry harder than anyone in the world. You often care more about my work than I do, which only makes me work harder. There's no way I'd be where I am—with you, Roxy, and Millie—or have the career that I do if you weren't the person you are. You are supportive and caring and kind. Thank you for being my husband and my best friend.

INDEX

Note: Page references in *italics* indicate photographs.